Don't Force It, Solve It!

Don't Force It, Solve It!

How To Design Meaningful and Efficient Design Processes

George Kalmpourtzis

CRC Press
Taylor & Francis Group
Boca Raton London New York

CRC Press is an imprint of the
Taylor & Francis Group, an **informa** business

First edition published 2022
by CRC Press
6000 Broken Sound Parkway NW, Suite 300, Boca Raton, FL 33487-2742

and by CRC Press
2 Park Square, Milton Park, Abingdon, Oxon, OX14 4RN

© 2022 Taylor & Francis Group, LLC

CRC Press is an imprint of Taylor & Francis Group, LLC

ISBN: 978-0-367-50589-9 (hbk)
ISBN: 978-0-367-50565-3 (pbk)
ISBN: 978-1-003-05044-5 (ebk)

DOI: 10.1201/9781003050445

Typeset in Minion Pro
by codeMantra

To my grandpa George

Contents

Acknowledgments xi

Author xiii

CHAPTER 1   If Only There Was a Way to Make Design
             More Efficient... 1

SECTION I   Don't Force It, Solve It!   5

CHAPTER 2   Processes, Humans, and Design 7

2.1   Processes, Humans, and Design 8
2.2   There Is Not a Universal Recipe for Creating
       Design Processes 21
2.3   All I Am Asking for Is 1 Hour. 24
2.4   So, What Is This Book About? 32

CHAPTER 3   The Biggest Design Secret **33**

3.1   The Form of Process 34
3.2   There Is No Design Process without a Problem
       to Address...39
3.3   The Biggest Design Secret.........................43

CHAPTER 4   The Human-Centered Process **57**

4.1   Processes Focus on Humans 58
4.2   Processes Should Encourage Creativity 59
4.3   Processes Entail but Tame Chaos 65
4.4   Processes Should Embrace Error 68
4.5   Process Should Maintain Team Stability 71
4.6   Processes Should Focus on Enabling Creativity Rather
       Than Creative Delivery.............................72
4.7   Processes Should Have Memory 72
4.8   Processes Should Encourage Personal Development 74

CHAPTER 5   Let's Make a Process **77**

5.1   What Type of Process Do You Want to Make?..........78
5.2   Processes Encourage Both Analytical and
       Synthetical Thinking...............................80
5.3   Problem Finding and Problem Solving 82
5.4   Activities, Activity Sets, and Broader Processes.........84
5.5   Processes Offer Different Levels of Focus 87
5.6   Process Structure Depends on Team Size 91
5.7   Processes Vary in the Number and Granularity
       of Steps 94
5.8   Processes Can Have Different Scalability
       and Adaptability 100
5.9   Processes May Consist of Different Phase and
       Step Sequences....................................102
5.10   Processes Are Human-Centered.....................106
5.11   Design Processes Focus on Feasibility and
       Encourage Innovation 109

5.12 Processes Should Incorporate User Research and Help
      Establish a Collective Memory 110
5.13 Processes Break Silos and Encourage Co-creation. 114
5.14 Processes Focus on Short- and Long-Term Outcomes
      and Have Different Durations 117
5.15 Processes Take into Account Organizational
      Complexity but Don't Reinforce It 119
5.16 Design Processes Improve the Efficiency of Already
      Established Processes 122
5.17 Processes Present Mitigation Strategies 123
5.18 Representation and Form. 124

CHAPTER 6   **The Process Core** **129**

6.1   Five Important Questions 130
6.2   The Process Core 143

CHAPTER 7   **Don't Force It, Play!** **147**

7.1   Play Is a Serious Matter 148
7.2   Design Processes Should Be Intrinsically
      Motivating 154
7.3   So, What Is Play? 156

CHAPTER 8   **An Introduction to Team Dynamics** **163**

8.1   Teams Are Built, Not Designated 165
8.2   Teams Consist of Creative Stakeholders. 168

SECTION II   The Design Process
             Rectangle   177

CHAPTER 9   **How to Read This Section** **179**

CHAPTER 10   Phase 1 – Finding and Understanding Problems . . .183

10.1   Problem Finding Is an Exploratory Process 184
10.2   Facilitating Problem Finding 185
10.3   Design Processes Use Narratives 193

CHAPTER 11   Phase 2 – Coming Up with Problem-
Solving Strategies 199

11.1   Divergent Thinking Strategies and
Design Processes 200
11.2   Convergent Thinking and Design Processes 215

CHAPTER 12   Phase 3 – Applying and Exploring Solutions 225

12.1   The First Step in Solution Application and
Implementation Is Communication 226
12.2   Exploring Different Solutions 229

CHAPTER 13   Phase 4 – Assessing Solutions and Processes 233

13.1   Solution Assessment 234
13.2   Process Assessment 245

SECTION III   The Creative
Stakeholder's
Journey   247

CHAPTER 14   The Final Chapter 249

References 253

Index 257

Acknowledgments

Writing a book is like embarking on a journey: you may know the destination (or at least you think that you do), but the path isn't always that clear. Some journey aspects may be rather straightforward, and some others may challenge your perspective, approach, and understanding of your professional, and broader, world. In order to embark on such long and exciting journeys, one needs the support of a team of brave and skilled heroes: working collaboratively, overcoming obstacles, and growing together. This section is dedicated to those who supported, impacted, and contributed to the creation of this book. Without the support and feedback of those heroes, this book would have never been written:

- George Ketsiakidis, Lazaros Vrysis, Margarida Romero, Fragkiskos Katsimpas, Christophoros Nalmpantis, Tilemachos Kalmpourtzis, David Jeanne, Remi Taieb, Ryan Gerber, Tobias Moller for their positive energy, feedback and for challenging my views and ways of thinking.

- Ifigeneia Tsolaki for her continuous and tremendous support in editing this book, encouragement, and colossal patience.

- Marcus O'Connor for his fantastic proof-reading skills and his infinite positive energy.

- Sophia Spyrliadou whose majestic designs make this book both easier to read and a visual delight.

- Sean Connelly, Jessica Vega, and all the great team at CRC Press without whom this book would have never been published.

- Margarida Romero, whose work and support has been instrumental on my research journey.

- All the amazing teams, colleagues, and friends all around the globe whom I have worked with throughout the past years, who have helped me grow and approach design through a broader and more human perspective.

Thank you for all these amazing memories!

Author

George Kalmpourtzis is an award-winning User Experience & Learning Experience Consultant and Game Designer. Finding himself between the fields of educational technology, design, and game studies, he has been founder, C-level stakeholder, director, and board member of several design studios, startups, and consulting agencies.

George has worked on a diverse portfolio of projects and contexts, spanning from highly complex dashboards to video games and from XR interfaces to mobile apps. He is currently helping L&D, design and product teams around the globe set up efficient and fun creative processes and bring user-centered creative problem solving in the heart of design. George also holds bachelor's degrees in both education and engineering, a master's degree in information systems, and a PhD in design pedagogy. He has created, taught courses, and given lectures in academic institutions and corporations all over the world.

Chapter 1

If Only There Was a Way to Make Design More Efficient...

DOI: 10.1201/9781003050445-1

- Frustration abounds among the User Interface (UI) designers, User Experience (UX) designers, and user researchers of a large corporation's design team. Even though they all want to contribute to creating great products, they consider that their voices are not being heard inside the organization. On top of that, the only things that seem to get created are obstacles, such as:
    - Dependencies with other teams (developers, analysts, product managers)

○ Deadlines that don't really take into account the time and complexity of the features they're meant to deliver

○ Mountains of change and feature requests that don't actually improve customers' final experience

As design is a complex process with lots of moving parts, the team feels their work and contribution are underrated. Some team members have the impression that the team only functions as a graphic assets "jukebox" for the organization. Others feel bored or frustrated, with the rest already searching for newer and funnier opportunities somewhere else.

• There's a communication breakdown between the development and design teams of a startup. Developers are passionate about creating robust mobile apps, but they feel that designers aren't approachable when they have questions about mockup designs and that proper documentation is often missing. To make things worse, as they rarely communicate with designers, developers aren't thrilled about all the design changes being made to interfaces they've already coded. They feel that designers switch up designs for no obvious reason and according to no particular logic. Designers, on the other hand, feel that updates to their designs are slow to be implemented or even never get done at all. They've got the impression that all developers ever do during meetings is slap unreasonable restrictions on their designs, which severely impacts their design output and the overall user experience.

• A large multinational corporation consists of dedicated development, design, user research, quality assurance, marketing, and product teams. Some of them are located around the globe making remote communication a key aspect of teams' workflow. This causes major coordination issues as each dedicated team communicates very little about their work, goals, and progress. There are times that design and development teams work on tasks that are set by product management, without actually understanding how they fit into the broader picture of the organization and its products. The outcome is that team tasks often overlap and at other times design proposals and technical stack configurations don't match, rendering several months' work obsolete. Everyone agrees that these errors could have been avoided if they didn't work in silos. However, the various teams are reluctant to take the initiative to improve communication as other teams may see that as an effort to take them over. Eventually, stakeholders are frustrated and all the teams blame each other for delays, rollbacks, or failed products.

- A large organization is experiencing an Agile at scale transformation. Even if the configuration, topology, and interaction between development, DevOps, QA, and product teams are rather clear, this isn't the case for the design teams. Designers are frustrated since they need time and resources to explore and test different design hypothesis. On the other hand, product and development teams have difficulty refining, estimating, and planning their work, due to this misalignment with the design teams. Both sides are unhappy.

If only there was a way to make design more efficient and the life of both stakeholders and users better...

Don't Force it, Solve it!

Chapter **2**

Processes, Humans, and Design

DOI: 10.1201/9781003050445-3

2.1 Processes, Humans, and Design

I talk to teams and organizations all the time that have lost faith in design, user centricity, and setting up their own design processes and activities. The main argument I hear is that they've already invested tons of time and resources but haven't seen the return on investment to justify it.

My answer is to remind them that:

It's not how much time we spend on design that impacts the final outcome: it's whether that time has been spent on solving the right problems.

Products that fail often have in common that they:

- Don't address customers' needs and expectations
- Present features and services that nobody cares about, so shouldn't exist in the first place
- Focus on pushing for new technologies, rather than delivering value for users
- Are a reflection of the organizational complexity in their creative environment
- Are difficult or complex to understand and use

We have tried setting up a process and it didn't work.
Did you do it right?

For every product or project that went wrong, there is always a team or organization that didn't function properly. It's quite common that behind unsuccessful products:

- There are teams that aren't working together harmoniously

- Coordination and a coherent vision are missing

- Communication among stakeholders gets difficult, causing frustration

- There is conflict that can't be resolved

- There is organizational complexity that stifles creativity and innovation

- Problem solving stagnates into a meaningless process, where stakeholders feel that their contribution has no value

Whether they realize it or not, design teams are often required to identify and solve business and user problems. However, no matter how frequently those problems may appear around the industry or in academia, each situation, organization, design team, and set of users come with their own individual particularities, making them unique.

This book puts both problem solving and problem solvers in the spotlight, aiming to help them address problem situations more efficiently. On this journey, we will examine some of the most popular design processes and identify their key characteristics so you can set up processes that meet the needs of your own design teams.

Before we get into the scope of this book any further, let's set a few things straight:

2.1.1 People Quit Design Teams and Processes That Are Boring and Meaningless

Technology evolves at warp speed. So, more and more competent professionals are needed across many industries. As a result, retaining talent and keeping it motivated becomes a huge challenge for all types of teams, from small startups to large corporations. Often, even if an organization offers lots of perks, people may still leave.

I believe that this is because we tend to forget that we (primarily and instinctively) search for **purpose, communication, and fun**.

If you go through your favorite memories, both personal and professional, the moments that you fondly remember and cherish are never dull or unenergetic.

On the contrary, those memorable moments were suspenseful. They entailed the element of surprise. They included exploration. They allowed us to have some type of control over an activity, to contribute, and to see the effects of our actions, whether we failed or not. They made us feel part of a group or a movement. This thrilling sensation is an integral part of great design teams.

It's not the challenge, bugs, necessary technical skills, or the very process of problem solving that scare people off: its dullness, communication problems, lack of control, and lack of interest.

2.1.2 Design Is Impacted and Driven
by Creative Stakeholders

Design, as a multidisciplinary field, takes into account user and business needs, technical resources, technological constraints, industrial environments, team dynamics, and many many more aspects. As a result, **directly or indirectly, every stakeholder of a product team contributes to the design of a product or a service**.

The multidisciplinary nature of modern product design requires harmonious collaboration between different types of experts, towards solutions that are **novel and original**. Both of these two attributes characterize creative individuals.

Contrary to popular belief, creativity is not a privilege of the few but a universal human trait. To make it even clearer:

Creativity is a skill that we all have. The more we work on it, the more skilled we become at it.

As a result, I don't believe that design is only driven and impacted by designers. In fact it's the opposite, **design is the sacred responsibility of all stakeholders who want to solve problems and create better experiences for their users and customers**. These people, whatever their background and technical expertise, are inquisitive, strive for originality in their field, and want to explore possible solutions for the problem at hand.

Hence, modern product teams don't consist of mere stakeholders: they consist of **creative stakeholders**.

Let's meet just some of them:

I want to be able to generate the maximum value for my products!

How can I efficiently work with development and design teams?

Louis, Product Manager
Paris, France

I Create User-Centered experiences that facilitate business goals.

How can I help my organization embrace user centricity?

Liz, UX Designer
Phoenix, AZ, USA
(working remotely)

I solve complex problems, Creating amazing gaming experiences for our players!

I help teams and organizations improve their Agile processes.

Mira, Game Developer
Singapore

Amanda,
Agile Coach
London, UK

I design intrinsically motivating learning experiences by Combining technology and pedagogy!

Josh,
Instructional Designer
Vancouver, Canada

2.1.3 Design Is about Intrinsically Motivating Problem Finding and Problem Solving

I often hear people explain that design is a problem-solving activity. Even if this statement is indeed correct, it manages to capture only half the essence of design: **Design consists of both problem finding and problem solving**.

Teams that get this point right are already half-way along the path to better performance.

Whether we realize it or not, in order to find and solve design problems, we incorporate a series of steps into our work methodology. The structure and order of these steps is based on training or experience. In other words, **whether it is structured or not, individuals and teams already apply some type of process in their design activities.**

I am absolutely certain that some of my colleagues will exhale sharply and roll their eyes when someone starts talking about process; and they might have a point. Processes can be highly effective, but they can also be cumbersome and frustrating. For many obvious and otherwise reasons, we won't focus on bad processes at this point. Instead, let's focus on some indispensable elements of what makes a good design process work.

One of the greatest misconceptions out there is that finding and solving problems is boring. I can say with great certainty that people who say that are absolutely wrong: **problem finding and problem solving are actually really exciting!** Let's take a moment to think back to our childhood days, when we were building playforts or putting toys together (and it's quite likely these moments weren't always brimming with success…). Back then we came up with design solutions, which were fun to propose and implement.

These experiences are still in our minds and hearts not only for their emotional value but also because of what they taught us. **These are the kind of design processes and activities we need: exploratory, intrinsically motivating, and, most of all, fun.** Such processes and activities need to capture our curiosity, allow us to contribute, provide freedom, and give us control during some of the steps, along with socializing, learning, and giving us the feeling that we are part of a group with a mission, where our views are heard and taken into consideration.

The fact that we need to create efficient and immersive experiences for our customers doesn't mean that making them can't be memorable for us at the same time!

Processes and activities like these motivate us: We want to partici-pate in them and contribute our energy and attention. We could also say that design **processes with these characteristics are**

autotelic, meaning that they have a purpose in themselves and there doesn't have to be another reason why we join them.

I prefer calling such types of processes and activities **intrinsically motivating design processes.**

Imagine people describing your workshops as meaningful and effective with everyone telling you what a great time they had and asking for more. This is the ideal design process.

2.2 There Is Not a Universal Recipe for Creating Design Processes

Fortunately, or unfortunately, there is no magic recipe for the establishment of successful design processes. Setting up a design process involves a perspective on various aspects that involve group dynamics, product design, organizational structure, change management, technical context, creativity, conflict management, communication, and the list goes on. All these aspects differ from company to company, from team to team, and from situation to situation. This also means that **a design process that works efficiently for a team at a given time may be obsolete for the same team for a different product, time, or context**. As a result, design processes are characterized by various approaches, structures, and forms.

There are currently several established and widely used processes for design, like the Double Diamond, Lean Startup, Design Thinking, or Design Sprints, which manage to address the needs and challenges of a variety of organizations. You are strongly encouraged to explore them and understand how they are structured. Each of them comes with many enlightening insights on process design that will help you understand how design processes are structured and set up.

However, no matter how well laid out these great processes are, they don't always fit particular organizational structures (whether simple or complex) and they won't always manage to address all the priorities, rhythms, team dynamics, resources, and other established processes that pre-exist within organizations.

As a result, teams and organizations either tweak and customize those existing processes according to their unique needs or set up their own design processes that better address and serve their needs. In either case, these processes need to be:

- **Effective**, successfully helping to achieve desired outcomes

- **Flexible**, able to adapt to altered circumstances and situations

- **Meaningful**, have some value for those who participate in them

- **Facilitating communication**, helping to eliminate ambiguity

- **Team building**, bringing together creative stakeholders, from the same or different specialties, and laying the necessary circumstances for them to understand each other, acquire a shared vision and co-create

- **Encouraging innovation**, embracing errors, taking risks, and encouraging exploration

- **Pragmatic**, taking into consideration different design situations and contexts

- **Constantly evolving** with the industry, customers, users, and organizations

- **Intrinsically motivating**, being both fun and having the element of surprise, rendering design a deeply enjoyable activity

- **Not focused on process for the sake of process** and steps but on people and the optimization of their work

2.3 All I Am Asking for Is 1 Hour

What I am asking for is 1 hour of a team's time. One hour during which the team will assess how happy and efficient they believe they are and see if and how they think they can improve their way of working.

What's stopping you?

If I had a nickel for every excuse I hear from stakeholders about why improving process isn't a priority, I'd be Bruce Wayne by now. While cruising in my Batmobile and rocking a black cape sounds cool, I still think that improving design processes should nearly always be top of the design to-do list. So, I decided to list some of the most common excuses I have encountered as food for thought:

- **Excuse #1: Our organization is too unique.**

  Working on design processes may seem like a daunting task for teams and stakeholders. They may feel that their established workflows, internal politics, and organizational complexity would be disrupted by a newly introduced design process. Furthermore, some stakeholders may consider that existing organizational complexity may not allow the establishment of a design process in the first place. I would point out that each and every organization is unique. However, organizations tend also to face similar challenges on some levels, such as embracing agility or user centricity. As a result, a design process that is conceived to address the unique challenges of an organization is beneficial.

designer

manager

- **Excuse #2: We just don't have the time.**
  This line supposedly renders any discussion about process moot. But design processes aren't established to slow things down, instead, they aim to speed things up. Working on

them shouldn't require infinite resources and dedicating a huge amount of time. Even small steps and adjustments can have a great impact on how a team works. Additionally, the return on investment on time for future iterations definitely makes improving one's design process worth it.

We have a new process that we would like to propose. It will make us more efficient.

This is a great idea. But... we've got deadlines piling up at the moment and there's just no time to do it.

Let's talk about it some other time.

designer

manager

- **Excuse #3: I think we've already found what's best for us and the team.**

   Change isn't always easy. Even if sometimes it makes our lives easier, we need to experience change so that we can see its impact on the way we work. Efficient design processes are those created or co-created by the people who participate in them. These people also manage change, making their creation and application smooth for the teams that adopt them.

- **Excuse #4: Reviewing our design process is just too expensive.**

   It's a huge myth that working on design processes needs tons of resources. Improving or establishing a design process only requires a team motivated to improve how they do design. Even a few steps and actions discussed over a coffee break can create positive change in how teams work.

- **Excuse #5: The blog article.**

   There is always a blog article that can be used as a counterargument for any proposal, solution, or idea. There will always be alternatives to doing or not doing things. Taking into account though that each team, project, and context are unique, creative stakeholders need to find the optimum configuration that will help them perform, enjoy, and deliver solutions to the problems they face.

- **Excuse #6: Setting up a design process may disrupt the balance between inter- and intra-team dynamics.**

     Contrary to this belief, establishing design processes may provide the opportunity for discussion and resolution of issues inside and outside creative teams. Later on, we are going to examine how to handle potential conflict while designing one's process and how to approach team dynamics.

These are often very valid arguments that, as we'll see throughout this book, need to be taken into account when setting up a process.

It's also true that **revolution doesn't just happen from one day to another** but requires the involvement and reflection of several actors in order to succeed. As we will see later on, setting up a process may initially raise concerns or friction between teams, since process is also connected to change (and change isn't always easy to deal with!).

It is important to point out that **not all teams or organizations need to change their way of working. Especially, if they feel that it won't bring any extra value or meaning to their work and user research supports their view.**

On the other hand though, **there are teams that face challenges that could be dealt with effectively if an efficient process was put in place.** In this case, effective and meaningful design processes are a game changer.

You don't really know if and which design process is best for your team until you try.

But how do we know if and when processes are effective and meaningful? We really don't, unless we test them in practice. As we will see in depth later on, design processes are living organisms that adapt to the needs of teams and organizations. Some of the positive characteristics of effective design processes include:

- Building strong teams and teams are stronger than heroes.

- Encouraging multidisciplinary perspectives where different experts gather together to design and co-create.

- Helping teams avoid errors early on in product and service development by applying iterative approaches.

- Facilitating and encouraging communication between different creative stakeholders inside and outside teams.

- Managing conflict by focusing on creative stakeholder relationships and team dynamics.

- Encouraging a culture of exploration and innovation where different team members engage in creative problem solving.

- Removing the ambiguity associated with design by helping teams to navigate complex systems.

- Embracing error as a fundamental aspect of design. Error is inevitable and valuable as it provides us with opportunities to learn.

- Encouraging exploration and out of the box thinking but, at the same time, eliminating chaos by proposing common channels of communications and shared tools, methodologies, and vision among different team members.

- Placing user and organizational needs at the center of design. For that reason, design processes facilitate, encourage, and disseminate user research.

All we need to get you there is 1 hour.

In order to solve a problem, a team needs to understand there is one. So, the 1 hour is the first step towards reflection and potential improvement of their work environment.

2.4 So, What Is This Book About?

As you have already figured out, this book aims to help teams establish their own efficient, meaningful, human-centered, and intrinsically motivating design processes. In order to do this, we are going to explore existing design processes and examine whether and how they can be adapted to different design contexts. We are also going to analyze those processes, identify their key components and attributes, and see how they can be used in order to create new, customizable processes, based on the individual needs of each team, organization, and context.

By reading this book, a creative stakeholder or a team will be introduced to a variety of processes, tools, and approaches that they can use. Additionally, they can build their own, customized design process, based on their particular needs, challenges, and issues.

More specifically, **after reading this book, you will have a better understanding of:**

- Setting up and encouraging creative problem solving for your teams, impacting design in your organization.

- Creating your own design processes, customized to your teams' needs, resources, and priorities. These processes can span from a 1-hour workshop to long-term design processes adopted by one or more teams in your organization.

- The subtle art of team building and team dynamics, a key component of any successful design process.

- Maintaining and keeping your process alive, up to date, and evolving based on the needs of creative stakeholders and your organization as well as your customers and users.

- Establishing collaboration and communication between the different teams, stakeholders, and divisions of your organization.

Chapter 3

The Biggest Design Secret

DOI: 10.1201/9781003050445-4

3.1 The Form of Process

Processes can sometimes have bad connotations and be associated with conflict, boredom, long and cumbersome discussions, office politics, or inefficiency. We may also have had an experience where an established or applied process has let us down.

What if I told you that, under the right circumstances, designing and participating in design processes is both fun and effective?

As we saw before, processes can be either highly effective or considerably troublesome, depending on how they're structured, used, or introduced. I will also point out that if we examine the most common current design approaches, we will see that they incorporate and propose processes that address the problems of the issues raised above.

3.1.1 Processes Consist of Activities

As we will see later on, there are various different structures and configurations for design processes. In all of these cases, however, **design processes consist of series of steps and each of those steps comprises individual or collaborative activities**. Let's look at some examples:

- In Agile software development approaches, a daily standup is an activity incorporated into the broader design and development process. Each team member describes tasks they worked on previously, what tasks they are going to work on, and what challenges they face.

- A brainstorming activity is part of a broader ideation and design process where stakeholders want to define a problem, brainstorm solutions, and choose a few of those proposals to explore further.

- An ice-breaker game is a short activity of a broader team-building process.

- A card-sorting activity is part of a broader exploratory process where UX designers want to identify the optimum configuration for their website's navigation.

As a result, we could break design processes down to activities like this:

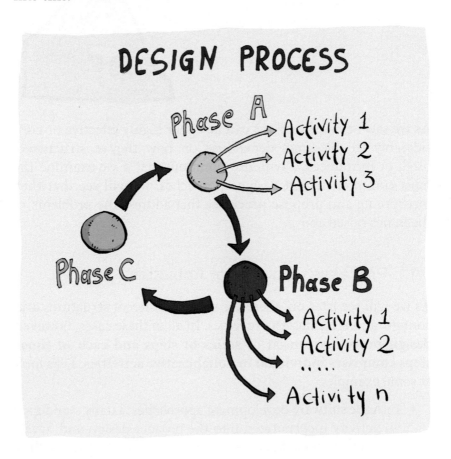

3.1.2 Activities Consist of Processes

We can also approach the relationship between process and activities from exactly the opposite direction too: **design activities are structured on different forms of process**. Let's see some examples:

- An ideation workshop, where people are gathered to work on potential solutions to a given situation, consists of steps where participants first propose a plethora of ideas and then narrow them down to a few that they consider more appropriate for a specific context.

- Usability tests, which present users with interfaces that creative teams have designed, are based on a series of steps. For example, during a usability test, the researchers who conduct the test will provide instructions about the session, they will present the designed interfaces to participants and provide them with some tasks to complete, while they take notes, and at the end, they pose follow-up questions regarding users' actions and perception.

As a result, we could potentially identify processes inside activities, like this:

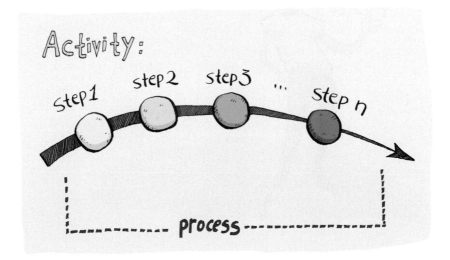

So, this interconnection between design processes and design activities can be approached as examining the two sides of the same coin.

This duality provides us with a great reflection tool, where **we can examine activities as part of greater processes and also processes as components of the activities that we want to create.**

For this reason, in this book, we will examine both how we can create design activities that can last for as little as 5 minutes as well as design broader design processes, both in terms of time and scale.

3.2 There Is No Design Process without a Problem to Address

Whether defined or otherwise, design processes address society, customer, and business problems. Not all problems are the same however, which calls for totally different courses of action depending on the situation. The first step to solving problems is to be able to identify and categorize them, giving us the opportunity to see which tools can be used to address them.

One way to categorize and address problems is into existent, emergent, and potential issues [1]:

- **Existent problems** are apparent and, in several cases, have even been previously identified and formulated by someone else. Often existent problems present an obstacle or a negative impact that needs to be overcome to arrive at a desired state. For instance, a usability issue which was spotted during a usability test is an existent problem: the problem has already been identified and formulated and a potential solution needs to be proposed and applied.

- **Emergent problems** on the other hand haven't yet been formulated, even if their existence may be potentially apparent to the solver after some investigation. We encounter emergent problems almost every day, like a drop in conversion rates, a decrease in the average revenue per user, users exiting a purchase funnel at a specific point, or an increase in task completion time for a new software update. In all those cases, even if a blocking point is observed, the very problem that causes this effect hasn't yet been identified and formulated. Designers need to dig into analytics or request user research in order to find the problem and then try to solve it.

- **Potential problems** haven't yet been formulated and haven't even been identified as potential problems. The identification and formulation of potential problems is the result of the synthesis of various elements which, in the eyes of problem solvers, could constitute a problem or an idea worth exploring further. Potential problems for instance can be new features of an existing product or a proposal for new products, based on environmental scanning and an analysis of customer needs.

We can also approach and describe problems as being **well- or ill-defined**:

- There are problems that are identified and solved as a result of an action or progress towards a desired situation being blocked [2]. In such situations, problems are already **well-defined** and their goals, solution path, and any potential blocking points are already identified [3] or can potentially be identified.

- There are problems which can be expressed as questions for inquiry [2]. Such problems are **ill-defined**, since we do not yet have a clear picture of our goals, available information, the resources at our disposal, or a solution path [4]. Ill-defined problems may also be rather complex and present various smaller problems and ways to solve them as well as varying in how they are formulated and approached. There are even occasions where a solution to an ill-defined problem may change over time depending on the context in which it's being addressed. For instance, "Addressing the impact of climate change" is an ill-defined problem, since it's rather complex, needs further definition, the approach to the problem is different for experts, scientists, and individuals from different industries, nations and expertise and the solution to the problem will highly likely be different depending on when we try to solve it.

It happens rather often that teams try to solve different types of problems, using the same tools and approaches. In the same way that we don't use the same screwdriver on different types of screws, we won't use the same approaches, processes, and activities for different types of problems. So, before we try to solve a problem, we will first try to identify it, define it, and see what tools are best for dealing with it.

In the same way that we don't use the same screwdriver on different types of screws, we won't use the same approaches, processes and activities for different types of problems.

3.3 The Biggest Design Secret

I'll cut right to the chase.

What I am going to tell you isn't new; it is however the most important point that you need to keep in mind when establishing your own design process. Every single creative problem-solving methodology, approach, and activity that you have ever used and participated in are based on the same principle, consisting of the following **Four Fundamental Phases**:

- A problem is found and understood
- Strategies to solve the problem are proposed, materializing into solutions
- Solutions are applied and explored
- The solutions as well as the process of coming up with them are assessed

If we were to represent these Four Fundamental Phases in an iterative manner, they would look like that:

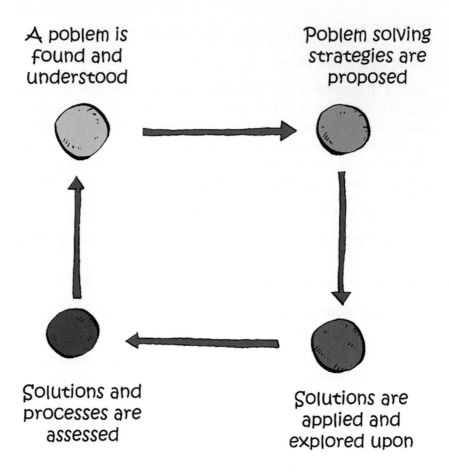

A poblem is
found and
understood

Poblem solving
strategies are
proposed

Solutions and
processes are
assessed

Solutions are
applied and
explored upon

Let's call this structure and framework the **Design Process Rectangle**. This is the result of decades of wisdom stemming from the work of great minds in the fields of education, psychology, mathematics, science, engineering, and the arts. In order to understand those steps, let's have a brief look at some influential approaches to creativity as well as problem finding and problem solving.

3.3.1 Some Theory and References behind the Biggest Design Secret

3.3.1.1 Dewey's Model of Problem Solving and Wallas' Four Stages to a Creative Process

One of the earliest and most influential contemporary models around problem solving and creativity was put forward by American educator John Dewey [5], who proposed the following steps:

1. A difficulty or issue is perceived
2. The problem is located and defined
3. Different potential solutions are proposed
4. The implications of each solution are assessed
5. One of the solutions is selected and evaluated

Psychologist Graham Wallas later on proposed another description for creative processes, consisting of the following four steps [6]:

1. **Preparation**: an individual or a team thinks about a problem, collecting information, and considering potential solutions.
2. **Incubation**: mulling over the problem while doing other activities. This can be anything from having lunch to taking a walk to one's morning shower, always with the problem in the back of one's mind.
3. **Illumination**: the moment when the solution appears. This solution is the result of the previous two steps, where all previous experience and information crystallize together in a way that highlights the solution.
4. **Verification**: the proposed solution is assessed in terms of validity and efficiency, along with other important factors.

In 1865 German chemist August Kekulé was trying to define the formula of benzene.

Even though the empirical formula of benzene was already known, scientists were still in search of its chemical structure.

One day though, Kekule daydreamt of a snake that had seized hold of its own tail, helping him come up with the benzene ring structure.

Kekule entered his preparation phase when he started trying to find the structure of benzene. His incubation phase was when he started daydreaming, while his illumination phase came just before the dream ended.

He now had a solution for the formula, which he could later verify.

Both these models approach creative problem solving from two different aspects: Dewey's approach focuses on the very process of problem solving and the outcomes of selecting and applying one solution method over another. On the other hand, Wallas' model focuses on problem solving through the prism of creative problem solvers, hence elaborating on how creative minds approach problem finding and problem solving.

3.3.1.2 Torrance's Process Model of Creativity

Another interesting creative process model has been proposed by psychologist Ellis Paul Torrance [7], which consists of the following steps:

1. A problem is sensed
2. Hypotheses or guesses about the problems are made
3. Hypotheses are evaluated, leading to potential revisions
4. Results are communicated

Torrance's approach entails a very interesting aspect: the communication and presentation of one's ideas and solutions. It is one thing to be a creative and avid problem solver and it is a totally different story to be able to present your thoughts to others and help them understand what they are.

3.3.1.3 George Polya's Problem-Solving Process

A very important contribution to problem solving is the work of mathematician George Polya [8] who, in his influential book *How to Solve It*, proposed a problem-solving process consisting of four steps:

1. **Understanding the problem**, where a problem is identified and understood
2. **Devising a plan**, where a solution plan is proposed
3. **Carrying out the plan**, where the plan is executed
4. **Looking back**, where the proposal and application of the proposed plan are evaluated

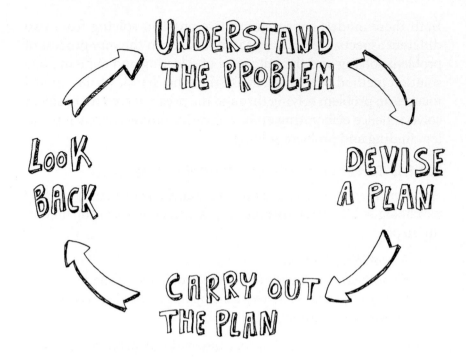

3.3.1.4 The Osborn-Parnes Creative Problem-Solving Model

Another interesting model, trying to both analyze and also improve creative problem-solving processes, is the Osborn-Parnes Creative Problem-Solving (CPS) model [9], the most recent iteration of which consists of four stages:

a. **Clarify**: teams explore the goals and challenges they have, collect and analyze data in order to define the problems they need to address, and formulate challenges to start searching for solutions.
b. **Ideate**: teams generate ideas, aiming to address the problems defined during the previous step.
c. **Develop**: teams propose concrete solutions, which are assessed for their feasibility and how they fit the situation, available resources as well as their impact when applied.
d. **Implement**: the team formulates their plan and examines what actions are needed to implement their solution, as well as examining how this plan will be accepted inside an organization.

3.3.1.5 The Double Diamond Framework

In 2004, the Design Council presented an innovation framework, aiming to address complex design problems, also referred to as the Double Diamond [10]. This framework is represented in the form of two rectangles (or diamonds). Each diamond introduces opportunities, first for divergent thinking, during which designers explore issues at greater depth or through various perspectives, and then for convergent thinking, during which designers take more concrete and focused actions.

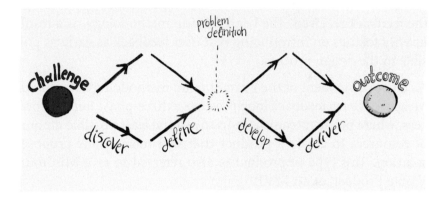

The Double Diamond describes four phases, which are:

1. **Discover**: During this phase, designers and nondesigners take time to better understand the problems they need to solve, gathering information about the organization, their customers, users, competition, or any other important factor that will later help them come up with some solutions.
2. **Define**: Collecting different types of information from various sources eventually culminates in the definition of problems that need to be tackled by the design teams.
3. **Develop**: Based on previously defined problems, multidisciplinary teams (including designers and nondesigners) come together, seek inspiration, brainstorm collectively or individually, and co-create in a participatory manner.

4. **Deliver**: Since teams have come with a plethora of solutions during the Develop phase, at this phase, these solutions are tested. Solutions that don't work are rejected, while others are improved.

3.3.1.6 The Build–Measure–Learn Feedback Loop

The Build–Measure–Learn feedback loop is a problem-solving framework proposed by Eric Ries in his work on the Lean Startup [11]. The Lean Startup methodology focuses on getting quick and actionable results on products and services through obtaining real feedback as soon as possible and revising one's strategy based on the feedback received. The Lean Startup methodology, as a result, heavily focuses on introducing real user feedback as early as possible in the design process.

As a key component of the Lean Startup methodology, the Build–Measure–Learn feedback loop presents a three-phase iterative process, where product teams aim to invest the least possible amount of resources to create a product that will reflect their proposed solution. This type of product is also referred to as a Minimum Viable Product, or an MVP.

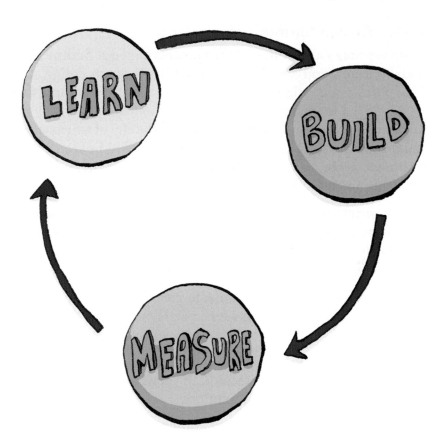

As its name suggests, the Build–Measure–Learn feedback loop consists of the Build, Measure, and Learn phases, which describe an iterative process where teams try to:

- **Build** their MVPs, based on the information, resources, and strategies they have.

- **Measure** their impact on users as well as their viability and sustainability from a business standpoint.

- **Learn** through their successes and failures as well as all the information and experience they gathered throughout the two previous phases.

Eventually, teams iteratively become more capable of reaching evidence-based business and design decisions.

3.3.1.7 Design Sprints

Design sprints started off as a 5-day process aimed at finding solutions to innovation and business problems through design [12]. This process was originally developed by Google Ventures and was designed to circumvent long debates and discussions by fitting months' worth of work into 1 week, by the end of which teams could come up with minimal products that could be tested with real users to see if the envisioned solutions work and are worth exploring and building upon.

Design sprints, being a great hit in the business and design worlds, have since evolved from a 5-day process to a six-phase process, which can still be run in more or less than 5 days, depending on team needs. These phases are:

- **Understand**: This phase aims to create a shared knowledge base across the stakeholders participating in the design sprints.

- **Define**: During the Define phase, teams assess what they learned and define the focus of the design sprint, the desired outcomes, and potential solutions.

- **Sketch**: This is an idea-generating phase, during which teams ideate both individually and collaboratively, trying to come up with solutions to the problems they have previously defined.

- **Decide**: Here teams agree upon the solution/s that are going to be prototyped and tested. This requires a synthesis of different ideas and establishing a consensus on which ideas are to be explored further.

- **Prototype**: The previously chosen ideas are prototyped. Issues are discussed and concept aspects are refined as the ideas are brought to life.

- **Validate**: At this phase, teams present their products to real users and see how they interact with them as well as observing their perception, disposition, and attitude towards them.

3.3.1.8 Design Thinking

Design Thinking is a problem-solving approach to design problems. Design Thinking has been developed over several decades [13] and became popular through the work of Stanford's d.school and IDEO.

Design Thinking presents an iterative, nonlinear, design process, the steps of which may vary depending on business and user needs. As a result, even if Design Thinking may be usually represented as a horizontal sequence of steps, design teams can jump backward and forward in any way that best suits their problem-solving process. Design Thinking has a strong user-centered aspect, focusing on prototyping and testing.

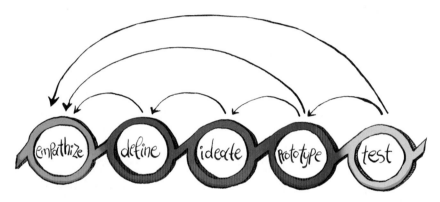

One of the different variations of Design Thinking consists of the following phases [14]:

- **Empathize**: During this stage, designers try to observe the behaviors and attitudes of their users, interact with them, and immerse themselves in the experiences of their users.

- **Define**: After designers have enough information and findings, they can transform them into compelling needs and insights, identifying what aspects can have meaning for their users. The result of this process is the statement of problems that design teams will later work on.

- **Ideate**: Ideation focuses on generating a multitude of concepts and outcomes and exploring a wide range of solutions both in terms of quantity and diversity.

- **Prototype**: The prototyping phase transforms idea/s into some sort of physical or digital form. This way, design teams can later test them with real users and get actionable feedback that helps them understand how to improve their ideas.

- **Test**: Here design teams aim to get feedback on the solutions they worked on. As a result, they can later refine them and continue to learn from their users.

Throughout the various models and processes proposed over the last hundred years, there is variation in the number of steps and particular focus regarding problem finding, problem solving, and creativity. However, several of these approaches and models consist of phases that are described by the Design Process Rectangle.

I find that four phases are a large enough number to lay out and analyze problem-finding, problem-solving, and creative processes in the scope of design but also short enough to present to creative stakeholders. Throughout the rest of this book, we are going to explore the Design Process Rectangle and its Four Fundamental Phases in detail.

What we need to clarify at this point is that:
Your design process doesn't necessarily need to consist of exactly four steps!

As we saw above, different approaches come with different types or numbers of steps. However, even if the configuration and sequence of steps may vary, the essence remains the same.

There are several factors and aspects that may affect the number of phases and steps of a process. As a result, **we will examine the number and configuration of the steps of your design process throughout this book.**

There are occasions for instance that the problem-finding phase may be broken into substeps in order to facilitate user research inside an organization or to help different team members better understand the problems they need to solve before actually looking for solutions. Similarly, there are situations where the Solution Proposing phase may be broken into more steps in order to take into account a team's brainstorming and idea selection procedures, as well as communication configurations, specific to their organization, such as discussion and exchange with stakeholders and other teams that have dependencies.

In other words, your ideal process may not necessarily consist of four steps: it may consist of more or less. However, no matter the number of steps, your process will need to take into account and incorporate the Four Fundamental Phases somehow. Lean

Startup, a widely used design process, for example, consists of the three phases of Build, Measure, and Learn. However, Lean Startup manages to merge the Four Fundamental Phases by breaking down its own main phases into smaller steps: The Build phase incorporates problem finding as well as coming up with problem solutions. The Measure phase incorporates both applying and experimenting with solutions as well as assessing the effectiveness of those solutions. The Learn phase on the other hand accounts for the reflection of both the proposed solutions as well as the improvement of process itself.

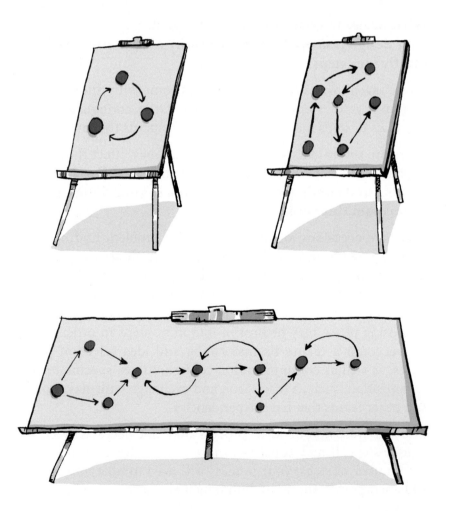

Chapter 4

The Human-Centered Process

DOI: 10.1201/9781003050445-5

4.1 Processes Focus on Humans

The basic ingredient behind every successful product or experience is the people that conceived and implemented them.

Meaningful user experience, efficient product strategies, spot-on user research, properly addressing customer needs, impeccable mockups, robust development, and immersion are all the result of the work of creative stakeholders and their teams. Great design solutions may affect users and customers as well as those around them. As a result, **creative stakeholders' work may have a great impact on cultures and societies**, changing people's lives for better or worse.

Without doubt, design is human-centered: it's a problem-finding and problem-solving process, conducted by humans for the benefit of other humans. As a result, design processes, being human-centered, should focus on their main ingredient: creative stakeholders.

It's important to point out that we are not born and raised in a vacuum. On the contrary, we continuously interact with those around us, we appropriate the information that we receive, and we continuously evolve in the context of the societies and groups we are part of. Design processes are no exception. By joining design teams, people interact with each other: they agree, argue, learn, co-create, support each other, and share memorable moments (both positive and negative). As a result, **design processes need to reflect these countless shades of humanity and create and orchestrate experiences that have meaning for creative stakeholders and help them to be more effective.**

So, how can we design processes that are human-centered? How can we help people socialize, exchange ideas, evolve, manage conflict, and perform altogether? Let's examine some key attributes of human-centered processes.

4.2 Processes Should Encourage Creativity

There are several ways, definitions, and approaches to creativity [15]. Without doubt though, creativity is always associated with these three major attributes:

- **Originality**: There are situations where we come up with proposals or ideas that we weren't aware of before. Even if we don't always immediately have the solution to some things, there are those "Aha!" moments that help us push our boundaries and propose novel solutions for solving the problems we face.

  Originality is continuously required in design contexts, where creative stakeholders need to come up with novel and original solutions to solve the problems they encounter. From proposing a new product to coming up with a solution that we haven't previously thought or seen, originality is a characteristic of creative stakeholders.

  Originality is both an individual and a contextual creativity attribute. For instance, people may propose features or products that for them are totally novel, while existing solutions may already be in place. Even if their proposals are original from their personal standpoint, they may not be for the broader audience or their team.

- **Appropriateness**: There is great debate about the definition of appropriateness in the scope of creativity. Let's look at why. During a training session some years ago, a participant proposed pushing an elephant out of a plane with a parachute as a way of promoting the activities of a local nonprofit organization. Her answer got me thinking. It was definitely an original idea; it hadn't been done before and the participant hadn't experienced something similar before. But was it feasible? And, as a result, was the proposal appropriate for the situation at hand?

The idea of a parachuting elephant as an advertisement trick would definitely be considered novel. But is it appropriate?

Several researchers and practitioners consider that originality, as a creativity concept, acquires its meaning inside the contexts of proposed ideas and solutions. This means that original solutions need to have some meaning and value in the context where they are conceived. Consequently, the notion of appropriateness can be relative to the context that is examined every time. What is very often a matter of debate, however, is how contexts are defined and where the limits of appropriateness actually end.

We experience the notion of appropriateness regularly in design when new technologies get no traction from consumers. Even if these new products propose novel features and functions, the technology may not be mature enough to generate proper value or users may not need or be accustomed to such a big disruption in their daily routines, especially if the proposed benefits are not that important. As a result, even if these proposals may be original and novel, they are not appropriate for their context.

- **Communication**: Throughout human history people have often engaged in creative activities to express themselves and communicate with others. Communication is an integral part of creativity for two reasons. The first is related to the fact that, since we are part of broader cultures and societies, our sources of inspiration, and consequently our creativity, stem from communicating and interacting with others.

  The second reason is based on our need and ability to express ourselves and communicate our creative thoughts. It is one thing being able to come up with creative visions and it's another to be able to express and present them to others. Creative ideas that are not presented or understood by others potentially have little value in design processes, where different creative stakeholders need to be able to communicate and align their mental models towards a shared vision.

Design history is full of examples and questions regarding originality and appropriateness, and creative stakeholders frequently face issues around originality, appropriateness, and communication in their work. As a result, design processes need to be able to address those aspects and guide creative stakeholders into communicating solutions that are both original and appropriate by providing visibility of the broader context to creative stakeholders and offering them tools that will help them express their ideas and vision to their peers.

In 1865 Jules Verne wrote a book called From the Earth to the Moon, talking about space travel, which at that period was an accomplishment achievable only in the scope of science fiction.

The definitions of originality, communication, and appropriateness change as we evolve along with the world around us.

Design processes need to be able to establish a fine balance in terms of pushing the limits of appropriateness and taking into consideration the context under which teams operate. Creativity is undoubtedly about pushing the limits of the possible and the unfeasible, the logical and the illogical and creating experiences that users haven't had before. But it's also about proposing ideas that have some meaning in the context for which they are conceived. The magic of establishing this fine balance is that it can shift the boundaries of the unfeasible and the illogical.

In other words, design processes that manage to both push the limits of teams' and users' understanding and structure of an experience, while maintaining balance between existing mental models and present limitations, manage to gradually make the impossible possible. We currently use technologies that just a few years ago we wouldn't have even dreamed of. Creativity, innovation, and technological evolution have pushed the boundaries of what was previously feasible, changing the way that we think and work, and leading to the adoption of new technologies in our lives.

4.3 Processes Entail but Tame Chaos

Encouraging and achieving originality is not a linear process. In fact, creative thinking can be rather arbitrary in the steps and directions it takes and that's normal. Unlike machines, human thought is based on various elements such as our brain structure, memories, experiences we have gained by interacting with our environment, the use of language, and our socializing with others.

So, instead of working like this:

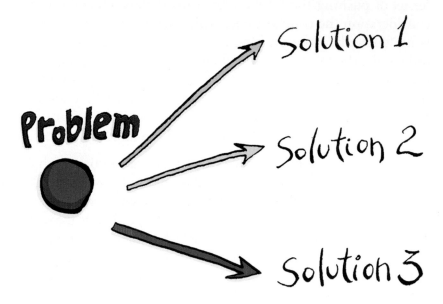

Humans think like this:

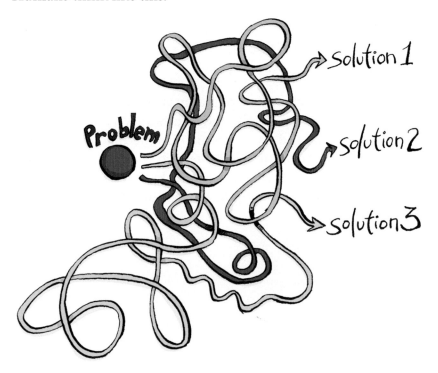

This very chaotic flow is the reason why some managers are afraid of creative processes since they feel (and in some cases they aren't wrong) that creative stakeholders may not be able to manage the process in terms of time or eventually measure its outcomes.

So, it's important to point out at this phase that **creative doesn't necessarily mean chaotic.**

Efficient design processes should be able to encourage and nurture creative thinking while also adapting to the pace that individuals, teams, and businesses need. There are various ways to do this by taking into account the creative flow of different teams, such as:

- Introducing dedicated activities, focusing on creativity and exploration

- Establishing specific opportunities for creative reflection in a broader process

- Iterative (and potentially incremental) cycles, where ideas may be explored

- Linear or nonlinear sequences of step taking, facilitating creative thinking and experimentation

We will look at all of these cases over the next chapters.

4.4 Processes Should Embrace Error

Failure is an unavoidable aspect of design processes. Creative stakeholders don't have psychic powers that allow them to see the future. Furthermore, they constantly need to make decisions based on unpredictable conditions and specific resources at their disposal. Some of these decisions may be successful and some may not as there are often unaccounted-for factors that aren't or can't be known. This is fine. Even more, this is a healthy step of design processes.

I'll put that last sentence another way: **not being able to accept error as part of a design process can actually turn catastrophic for organizations and their products**. There are organizations where the whole notion of error is a taboo. Consequently, this means that creative stakeholders may hold back from proposing ideas that have even a slight possibility of being wrong in fear of being judged harshly or losing future opportunities.

We already established that a fundamental pillar of creativity, and hence innovation, is originality. How do we expect creative stakeholders to propose original ideas, when they are afraid that they could be punished for them later?! Without being able to accept failure, teams won't take risks or try something new, they'll stay on the same path they started out on, wherever it's headed, overthinking any proposal for change out of fear of being characterized as a failure. This is wrong.

Instead, failure should be embraced and seen for what it is: an opportunity to learn and become better at what we do. Whether we understand it or not, we have actually applied this healthy approach right throughout our lives: When we fell over as toddlers, we'd stand back up and go again and do it better! When we tried to build a fort, we would learn from every time it would collapse and make it sturdier the next time! When we would fail at finding the right solution to a math problem, we would be shown how it's done again so we'd become capable of doing it ourselves! So, why change now?

The sooner we are able to confirm that one of our proposals has failed, the sooner we can focus on the next one that could be a better fit for the challenges that we face. Successful design processes should be able to convey this message both to the team members that apply them and also to the whole organization.

4.5 Process Should Maintain Team Stability

Conflict is often encountered in design contexts and processes. Efficient design processes try to manage and alleviate it, bringing stability and a positive atmosphere to design teams.

Inquisitive mindsets and a desire for innovation are aspects that should be encouraged in the scope of creative processes. When several creative stakeholders come up with various ideas, a discourse begins. I have been party to all kinds of such discourses: from the very calm or dull ones to some highly heated situations. As some people are attached to their ideas more than others, there will occasionally be conflict that needs to be managed, ideally through the tools and configuration of the design process itself. As we will see later on, ideation workshops and voting sessions are designed to deal with cases like these.

It is also normal that creative stakeholders, who have been through a creative process and have laid out their ideas, expect that their ideas will be considered and examined. There are situations where creative stakeholders are asked to come up with ideas, which are then not taken into account, either because the existing process (or lack of process) couldn't actually examine them or just because someone higher up the ladder decided that their idea didn't deserve more merit.

I find that no matter how attached people are to their personal ideas and proposals or no matter how strong-minded they may be, they are open to changing and accepting their views if the process is fair, clearly communicated, and inclusive. All the different aspects that we examine in this chapter build up to this very point.

4.6 Processes Should Focus on Enabling Creativity Rather Than Creative Delivery

More and more often I happen to join sessions where the facilitators, organizations, and teams have all sorts of amazing perks: from fancy stationery to slick digital aids and from really polished and animated slide decks to colorful bean bag sofas. These are all nice to have and I thoroughly enjoy (and am often thoroughly fascinated by) the creativity devoted to putting them all in place. But, to my disappointment, many of those sessions are rather boring and, in many cases, inefficient.

I find that there is a tendency to focus on creative deliveries and presentations rather than the very reasons the session is being run in the first place: to find problems and solve them.

Even if it is awesome to be addressing the Design Process Rectangle while drinking an iced Frappuccino Latte Macchiato with Extra Cinnamon, the fancy beverage won't define the outcome of the session. So, when designing creative design processes, think first and foremost of how you are going to address the challenges through trying to apply the Design Process Rectangle. After that you can look at, what I call, the sprinkles.

4.7 Processes Should Have Memory

A very common problem for large and small organizations alike is that when new people are being onboarded, senior team members realize they don't always remember why some decisions were originally taken, why legacy code or mockups are currently in use, and what studies, if any, have been previously conducted. **This is lack of process memory**!

Even if it sounds simple, several organizations don't manage to successfully maintain and pass on knowledge and information to those who need them. Unfortunately, in cases like these, answers to the problems and challenges regarding existing products can only be given by finding the people who actually designed and developed them in the past and hoping that they haven't already left the team or the organization.

Whether it's lack of organization, lack of priority, or lack of resources, organizations that fail at remembering their successes and failures, their customer needs and expectations, the evolution of their vision, and business value propositions are destined to repeat the same mistakes in the future. Taking the same road twice all the way to a dead end is a waste of time and resources.

As a result, design processes should encourage user research but should also be able to communicate, promote, and educate stakeholders about it as well as making sure to keep it alive.

4.8 Processes Should Encourage Personal Development

From the moment we are born, we embark on an amazing journey where we interact with our environment, our family, our friends, and our peers. We continuously assimilate information around us, converting it to knowledge that we can use, increasing our skills and competences. As a result, we constantly evolve. At every moment of our lives, we are learning something new.

Design, like any other human activity, requires that people learn and acquire new skills through which they can provide solutions to the problems of the field. On the other hand, the field of design continuously evolves as people, who learn by interacting and growing within the field, learn and acquire new skills, which they later pass on to their peers.

Learning is an indispensable aspect of human nature and has wrongly and unfairly been connected with boredom and dullness. In contrast to this, however, the element of fun is strongly related to how people learn. The most classic example is if we go back to our childhood where we would explore the world around us with great excitement. Finding out that water turns to steam when boiled or snow melts if you bring it inside were startling discoveries at the time. We wanted to learn more, and we were motivated to continue exploring the world around us because we wanted to quench our own curiosity. As a result, processes that help their participants learn are already on track to become intrinsically motivating.

Additionally, the field of design, following constant innovation, is flexible and adaptive to new contexts. As a result, organizations frequently request that their employees use newly introduced tools, get familiar with new methodologies, and apply recently developed skills. Consequently, learning becomes an integral part of organizational structure and, thus, creative stakeholders' lives.

However, learning within organizations may not always be efficient for a variety of reasons, including the inability to rapidly adapt to learning demand and needs, organizational complexity, lack of resources, lack of organizational interest in training and development or the use of learning tools that are not suited for organizations and their employees. This is why learning needs to be part of design processes in the first place.

Chapter 5

Let's Make a Process

DOI: 10.1201/9781003050445-6

5.1 What Type of Process Do You Want to Make?

Now let's get to work!

There are several aspects to creating design processes, and we are going to examine them all, one by one, in this chapter. Creating design processes has some similarities with cooking, in the sense that different recipes require the combination of specific ingredients. Just as we wouldn't add chicken to a chocolate chip cookie recipe, we need to pick what elements we need our design process to be made of.

So, the main question that you need to be able to answer is what type of process you want to make:

- Is it a long-term process about how your design team will work from now on?

- Is it a 1-hour ideation session you plan to facilitate with your peers?

- Is it about aligning your team's work with a newly introduced Agile framework?

- Is it a week-long workshop where you will need to come up with an initial product proposition?

Throughout this chapter there is a set of reflection tools, each of which has been proposed to guide you through the different elements that you can include (or not include) in your process.

Even if coming up with concrete, efficient, and actionable design deliverables remains one of the main reasons why we set up design processes in the first place, **focus should also be put on facilitating communication between both individuals inside teams and teams within broader organizations**. For instance, there is little value in setting up efficient design processes for design teams when their work won't be used or even communicated to the development teams, product managers, or higher-level stakeholders.

Processes need to focus on people and how they can co-create, deliver, and interact in their work environment. Design processes that are intrinsically motivating and fun to join have a much better chance of:

- Attracting more creative stakeholders

- Engaging them in creative problem-finding and problem-solving

- Helping them to communicate, exchange ideas, and learn

- Offering them memories that they will fondly look back on

As a result, design processes worth remembering make us better, help us grow, and make us more effective and efficient. Hence, through them we also succeed in improving performance and creating better experiences for our users and customers.

So, let's start examining the different elements and aspects of process one by one. These elements and aspects have been conceived to act as points of reflection when you create your own processes and activities. As you go through them, try to reflect upon how they relate to the processes and activities you want to create in your own specific contexts.

5.2 Processes Encourage Both Analytical and Synthetical Thinking

Consider an e-commerce website that suffers a massive drop in sales during a specific month. Compared to previous months and to the same month last year, the difference is considerable. The design team of the website, being curious, starts off by checking the site's analytics to try and identify what the issue could be. They also perform a quick benchmark of the site's competitors to see if any big offers had been put out that might have drained away their regular customers. Among other things, they scan their environment by reading blog articles, newspapers, and social media in order to identify any patterns or events that might have caused sales to drop on their site. So, the design team started their investigation by taking a problem (their e-commerce platform sold less compared to other periods) and then analyzed and broke it down into smaller parts, which they examined individually. **This is analytical thinking**.

On the other hand, there are many examples where design teams have to take into account a variety of elements, such as:

- Technical restrictions (like which technical stack is going to be used for a project)
- Business needs
- A particular target audience
- Competitor analysis

They are tasked with finding solutions where all these aspects are well bound together in a common and comprehensive solution. This process requires **synthetical thinking**, since individual components are synthesized together in a way that they make sense.

Both analytical and synthetical thinking are crucial for the creation of interesting and meaningful customer and user experiences. On the one hand, design processes need to offer creative stakeholders the space and resources to break down problems into smaller parts, making analysis and solution easier to implement. On the other hand, design processes need to help creative stakeholders to put all the different components and pieces of their work together, reminding them of the bigger picture and how all these individual parts contribute to making it happen.

REFLECTION POINTS

1. What problems will your design process solve?
   a. Should your design process break them down? If yes, into what components should those problems be analyzed?
   b. Are these problems part of a greater problem or system? If yes, what are the other elements that constitute those problems or systems?
2. Design processes often give creative stakeholders the opportunity to use both their analytical and synthetical thinking skills by breaking down problems and then synthesizing them into broader solutions. At which steps of your design process should analytical and synthetical thinking be encouraged?

5.3 Problem Finding and Problem Solving

We have already established several times that design processes need to facilitate both problem finding and problem solving. In order to achieve that, such processes need to establish an inquisitive mindset, which will help stakeholders identify and, later, solve problems. As we will see later on, qualitative and quantitative user research are very efficient tools that help with problem finding and problem solving. Changing habits, approaches, and perspectives in organizations takes time. As a result, establishing a problem-finding and problem-solving culture should be embedded in design processes early on.

Additionally, the activities that creative stakeholders will participate in should properly facilitate problem solving, allowing them to understand the given problems, analyze them, and come up with solution strategies.

REFLECTION POINTS

Teams participating in your design process should have a clear understanding of the context and problems they will be asked to design for.

1. Does your process provide creative stakeholders with enough information to proceed to problem solving?
2. What are the sources of information that your design process would present to creative stakeholders? Are there any quantitative (surveys, analytics, benchmark studies, etc.) or qualitative (usability tests, interviews, field studies, etc.) data that your process could provide?
3. Is the information provided by your design process up to date? If yes, how often does it get updated (if this is a long-term process)?
4. Does the design process give participants the opportunity, space, and time to find and propose other problems relevant to the context they address?

5.4 Activities, Activity Sets, and Broader Processes

As we saw in Chapter 1, there is a particular connection between processes and activities: activities can be based on processes and processes may consist of activities. This means that when we are asked to come up with our own design process, we need to take this special relationship between process and activity into account, based on our aims and needs.

Since simplicity is gold, we can narrow down the basics:

- **Activities**: Actions or sets of actions by creative stakeholders towards the accomplishment of goals. In this way, activities can be several things, including ice-breaking games, discussions between stakeholders, design proposals coming from one or more individuals, team-building sessions, or classic meeting sessions.

- **Activity sets**: Include more than one activity, orienting creative stakeholders towards the accomplishment of the same goals. It's important to clarify that not all creative stakeholders need to participate in all activities of an activity set. Activity sets, for example, could describe different types of brainstorming sessions taking place during one day of a 3-day design workshop. Another example of an activity set are activities aiming to find and define problems in the first place. For instance, a mobile app design team, based on research they conducted, could run an activity set, consisting of three activities, aiming at:

- Defining their primary user audience

- Identifying their users' needs

- Identifying potential problems that users may have when using their app

- **Processes**: Sequences of phases or steps aiming to achieve specific goals. Processes can have a wide array of different forms, focus, durations, and structure. They may consist of smaller processes or activities and, inversely, they can also be part of broader processes or be used as a basis for activities. The Design Process Rectangle is an example of a process.

REFLECTION POINTS

What type of activity or process do you wish to design? Is it a broad process? Is it an activity? Is it an activity set?

5.5 Processes Offer Different Levels of Focus

Design processes for different teams, audiences, and projects can be quite different. There are, for instance, processes that focus on the whole picture of products and services, offering a synthetic vision. Such types of processes may for example aim at creating a UX strategy for the organization, defining or redefining the business value of products, or establishing common workflows and communication channels between different teams.

There are also other types of processes that focus on individual components of broader systems, from the simplest visual component to more complex structures. An ideation session for example, where different stakeholders gather together to brainstorm and come up with solutions about the layout of a website's homepage, focuses on one component of a broader system: the homepage. There are of course processes that combine both a broader vision and individual parts of products and services.

I was once asked to organize a 3-day-long workshop, aiming to come up with an initial vision for an upcoming product. At the end of the workshop several participants expressed their discontent with the event because they lacked visibility on the product's technical limitations, available resources, and audience-related information. Their feedback was that, even if the workshop proposed brilliant insights, all the work that was accomplished during those 3 days could go to waste if our process lacked visibility on those key aspects.

We have gathered here today to define the vision for our website.
Do we have any user research? It will help us make our proposals.
Is there an existing design system that we can use?
designers
What technical stack are we going to use? Different stacks have different pros and cons.
Do we have any dependencies with other teams regarding the solutions we will come up with?
developers
This activity should help us get those answers, since we currently lack visibility on many aspects.

As a result, design processes should be able to provide clarity of the different levels or components of product and service design, providing creative stakeholders with a global overview of the problems and context they address. For example, a design process aimed at helping to define the product vision of an Augmented Reality headset should make sure that the creative stakeholders who participate in it have enough information about the individual components of the product (such as technical limitations, design trends, competitor analysis, user demographics, needs, and habits) in order to make informed decisions.

At the same time, processes that focus on smaller parts of a larger system or experience should offer visibility on the broader vision and help teams establish synergies, creating experiences that are consistent as a whole.

At the same time, processes that focus on smaller parts of a larger system or experience should offer visibility on the broader vision and help teams establish synergies, creating experiences that are consistent as a whole. Design processes that focus solely on a small part of a greater system or concept may lead to inconsistencies or misalignments and may impede decision making later on, since different teams may take different directions for the same project. This is an aspect often found in siloed organization structures, where different product teams work on a small part of a greater product. Even if these teams have established design processes on their own, the lack of a coherent direction and communication between them may lead to a mosaic of different solutions, very likely inconsistent, disrupting the overall final experience.

Some years ago, I was part of another project, where three different design teams came up with three different designs for the same components for their own products. By the time the organization realized this, the components had already been developed and released online, creating a very interesting, but highly incoherent, design experience.

So, design processes that focus on smaller parts of a greater organization should make sure that communication with other teams within the organization is strong and consistent.

REFLECTION POINTS

Design processes should provide visibility both on individual components of broader products and systems as well as the whole vision. However, they can also specialize on one more than the other.

1. How much visibility does your design process provide on the broader product vision?
   o Are there any activities or initiatives put in place in order to explain to creative stakeholders the organization's strategy and vision?
   o Is your target audience clear to creative stakeholders? Is user research about this audience shared?

o Are business objectives clearly communicated to creative stakeholders?

o Have you identified dependencies and communication channels with other teams? In this case, are there any elements and components that can be reused in your process?

o Are creative stakeholders aware of common tools, practices, and methodologies they can use?

o Are there any repositories with resources, research, or any other type of information communicated around the organization?

o Do different teams know what others are working on?

2. Are creative stakeholders aware of the individual components that your design process addresses?

o Are any technical limitations clear?

o Should creative stakeholders be made aware of the different aspects and components of the system you are working on and how would this be done?

o Are dependencies between products and systems presented to teams?

o Are there any studies regarding information architecture or system structures that would help creative stakeholders have a better understanding of the synthesis of the system you are working on?

5.6 Process Structure Depends on Team Size

Team size can have a big impact on the structure and creation of design processes. This is because team dynamics and communication are very different in teams of five people compared to teams of 50 people. It is, for instance, easier to facilitate communication and visibility within smaller teams: people who are less confident in expressing themselves in front of a large audience or those who avoid confrontation will also find it easier communicating in teams like this.

However, we also often need to create processes geared towards large teams such as:

- Centralized design team processes

- Alignment processes between different design squads in decentralized organization configurations

- Ideation and co-creation sessions with a large number of stakeholders

- Stakeholder workshops with a large audience

In these cases, the dynamics, communication, and mood of participants are very different as participants may not know each other or may be more reserved than usual and there's a big possibility that a few participants will dominate the conversation and drive the discussion. Deciding to create design processes for large teams requires lots of preparation and a developed set of facilitation skills and tools.

So, eventually, for every activity we design, we actually have to find a balance between inviting enough participants to help the design process advance and taking into account that the bigger the team, the greater the complexity in communication and team dynamics.

> ## REFLECTION POINTS
>
> What you need to take away from this reflection point is that the number of people that will directly (and potentially indirectly) participate in the process you want to create will definitely impact the communication, team dynamics, and output of the team.
>
> For more information and insights on this point, check out Chapter 8, "An introduction to team dynamics."

5.7 Processes Vary in the Number and Granularity of Steps

Not all processes come with the same level of detail. Some consist of few steps and provide a general perspective on addressing design, while some others are more granular, consisting of smaller steps. There are pros and cons to both types of structure.

Design processes that lay out broad phases (i.e. with less granularity) are easy to present and explain to stakeholders. Their simple structure can prove to be a great asset when trying to get buy-in from upper management, since the process is easier to explain to managers or C-suite stakeholders. On top of this, people can learn them more easily, since their simple logic is easy to follow. As a result, they can potentially be more easily adopted by team members.

Design processes with little granularity are also quite handy in contexts where we want to focus on broader design practices and guidelines rather than define more elaborate workflows. This can apply to both large and small organizations. Small startups for instance, whose structure and size may be rapidly scaling, may opt for processes with little granularity at the beginning, aiming to put in place their design principles and best practices, allowing design teams to flexibly define and redefine the individual steps for each process phase. There are very successful processes that are famous for their simplicity and efficiency. The lean startup approach for instance [11] is one of them, consisting of three phases: Build, Measure, and Learn.

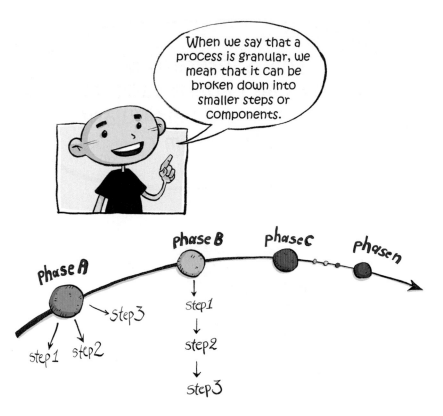

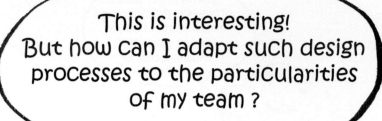

However, it can happen that processes that are not granular may be open to interpretation from different stakeholders, creating confusion or communication problems. The danger in this case is that their simplicity in presentation or structure may lead stakeholders to interpret and apply them differently according to their own point of view, leading to disparate process executions (or eventually totally different processes) even inside the same teams.

LITTLE GRANULARITY   GREAT GRANULARITY

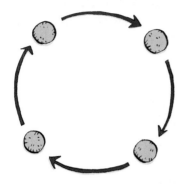

As we already discussed, there are processes with little granularity which may have been established based on a specific organizational structure, team size, or configuration of creative stakeholders. The problem with such cases is that teams grow in size, new people (with new ideas, habits, and needs) join and leave teams, and organization configurations change frequently to address business needs. As a result, conventions about how processes might work between existing stakeholders or teams may not always stay the same, making the application of little-granularity processes challenging.

In the ever-changing world of technology innovation, the state of teams shouldn't be considered a stable variable when creating a design process: on the contrary, potential evolution and change must be taken into account. Let's imagine a team following a design process with four steps, where its communication and interaction with other teams is not explicitly defined. Let's now consider that this team's company decides to change its organizational structure, getting more teams involved in the development and design phases (e.g. marketing, development, or consumer insights). It's very possible that potential interpretations of the existing process will cause disruption to the workflow of the teams involved, which will need to be addressed through a new or revised design process.

On the other hand, there are several occasions where more elaborate and granular design processes need to be put in place. Large organizations are a characteristic example as they feature:

- Organizational complexity

- Team interdependencies

- Existing and unavoidable protocols and procedures that can't be circumvented

- Team configurations with stakeholders of different specialties (e.g. having designers and developers on the same team)

This means that they require a more granular design process that addresses and brings solutions to the various challenges that teams already face.

Granularity is also related to the type of processes and activities that are proposed to creative stakeholders. Processes may propose general sets of steps, providing guidelines for team workflow, but they can also be concrete activities, like design critiques, ideation sessions, or week-long workshops, with specific steps. This topic will also be covered in the *duration and outcomes* reflection point later on.

A good balance between little and great granularity needs to be achieved for each context, case, and team. Efficient design processes should not reflect or reinforce organizational complexity; this goes against their very purpose. This doesn't prevent us, however, from proposing design processes with several (consecutive or nonlinear) steps that may address the particularities of a team, its position in the organization, and how the team interacts with it.

In cases like this, the Design Process Rectangle can start as an initial basis, which you can then break down into several more steps, each of which will address the issues that your particular organization may face. As we will see later on, these steps don't necessarily need to be linear.

REFLECTION POINTS

What level of granularity are you considering for your process?

1. How many steps will your process have?
2. What are the broader phases your process consists of?
3. Are these phases broken down into steps? If yes, what are those steps?
4. Who are you going to present this process to? Does your process presentation require a small or large amount of detail?
5. Do you need more than one level of detail (both broad phases and individual steps) for your process?

5.8 Processes Can Have Different Scalability and Adaptability

Not all processes can be applied in every situation or context. As we already saw, processes are based on humans, organizational particularities, available resources, team sizes, the objectives they need to achieve, and the list goes on.

The more focused and targeted a process is to specific teams and their particularities, the more efficient it is at addressing their individual problems and challenges. However, processes that were designed for a specific team configuration are not always easy to apply to other contexts, since they were originally conceived based on very specific parameters and with specific teams and people in mind.

Since work environments, team interactions, team members, size, and configuration are prone to change, we should definitely consider whether the processes we want to come up with are easily adaptable and scalable in a case where all those aspects change.

Processes that have the capacity to be scalable and adaptable are, on the other hand, more generic regarding the way they address individual team needs. Since they are conceived with the intention of being applied to a variety of cases, their structure focuses primarily on establishing a broader and more generic flow and set of steps, which teams and organizations will later adapt to their particular situation.

Design process scalability is important for both large organizations and startups that foresee growth mid and long term and plays a key role in the implementation of Agile at scale solutions and frameworks.

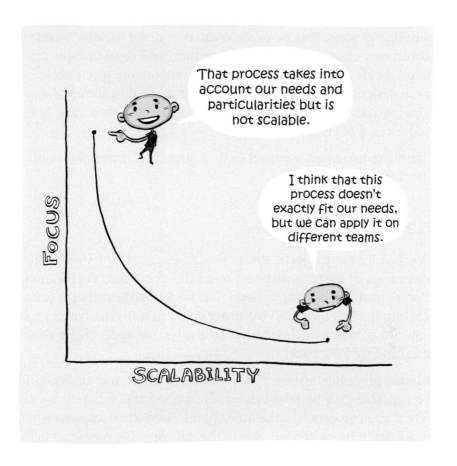

REFLECTION POINTS 🔍

How scalable and adaptable is the process you want to design?

- Is your process based on your teams' particularities (specific people, team configuration, team size, interactions with other teams, resources, organizational structure)?
- Will your process be used by different teams and in different contexts of your organization? In this case, is your process scalable for more and bigger teams?

5.9 Processes May Consist of Different Phase and Step Sequences

There is no definitive rule for the structure and configuration of a design process. Processes are created in order to solve business, consumer, creative stakeholder, product, and organization problems. As all these parameters are different on any given occasion, each design process may be different or applied in different ways. One of the main questions regarding process structure is the sequencing of phases and steps.

There are two main approaches to sequencing: linear and nonlinear. Let's examine both.

5.9.1 Linear Processes

As their name suggests, linear processes consist of well-defined sequences of steps, positioned one after the other. For example, Polya's problem-solving process that we looked at earlier is linear. During that problem-solving process, we initially analyze a problem, we come up with solution strategies, we apply those strategies, and we look back.

Linear processes are easy to present, explain, and understand. Hence, they can be relatively easily applied and followed by different stakeholders. On the other hand, there are occasions where more flexibility is needed, due to the nature of the problems being examined, organizational structures, and the different types of teams participating in the design process.

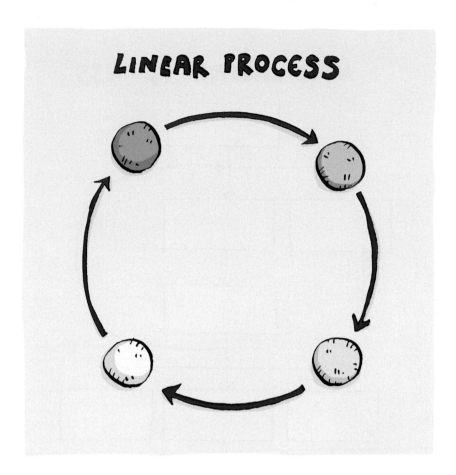

5.9.2 Nonlinear Processes

As design processes can have different levels of granularity, they may consist of few or many little steps, defining how teams interact with each other. In cases like this, process flexibility and the possibility to repeat some steps before moving forward, or potentially skip steps that may not apply for a particular iteration, are necessary to make the process viable and meaningful. In situations like this, **nonlinear** processes offer several advantages.

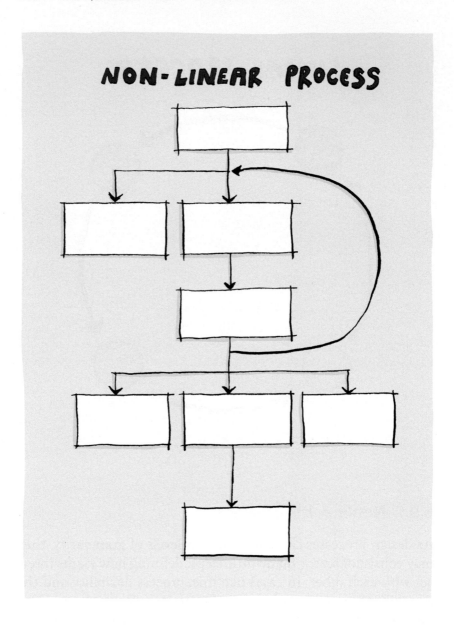

Nonlinear processes do not always follow a specific phase sequence but may incorporate different sets of steps depending on different situations. But nonlinear processes are still based on a logical phase structure. However, this logic doesn't dictate the same sequencing for every iteration. Design Thinking presents a very interesting nonlinear approach. The methodology consists of phases, broken down into steps, represented in a linear and sequential manner. However, Design Thinking specifies that from every step of the process, creative stakeholders can jump back to any previous step if they consider that revision or more information is required. As a result, Design Thinking has a strong nonlinear component, helping creative stakeholders adapt it to their needs.

Design processes should be robust in the sense that their structure should solve problems and remove complexity instead of creating them. As a result, steps that may on some occasions be redundant (due to lack of resources or interdependencies) should be optional in the design process configuration, so that they don't act as blocking points. On the other hand, steps that are indispensable for the process to advance and move forward should be made clear to creative stakeholders. As a result, necessary actions should be included in the process so that these steps are properly implemented when the time comes. For example, if a team decides that running usability tests after they propose a set of mockups is an indispensable step of their process, necessary time and resources should be allocated to conduct these tests. Additionally, the importance of this step should be made clear to any other creative stakeholders impacted by the established design process, such as project managers, product owners, or developers.

REFLECTION POINTS

1. Is your process going to be linear? If yes, what steps will it consist of?
2. Is your process progress going to be nonlinear? If yes, what are the steps it consists of and what are the potential sequences that the process may follow?
3. Are there steps and phases that may be optional? Have you identified them?
4. Are there steps that are indispensable for your process? If yes, which ones are they? Have you taken the necessary actions to communicate those steps to the stakeholders impacted by your process?

5.10 Processes Are Human-Centered

We have already established that design processes are human-centered. This means that these processes are conceived for creative stakeholders who design experiences for other humans. Consequently, when designing your process, you need to consider all the different people impacted by this process, directly or indirectly. Some of the questions you need to address are:

- **What users does your process target?**

   The more information we have about our potential customers and users, the more effective our process will be at addressing their problems and expectations. Depending on our team and organizational goals, the potential connection of our user base and outcomes on local groups, communities and societies could also be analyzed. In this way, we become more efficient at identifying and measuring the impact of our products on all those different actors.

   Even though we may think we know how our users think, feel, and act, one thing is certain: we are not our users! The best way to get information about our users is to meet and interact with them. A very powerful tool for getting information about our users is user research, which we will look at later on. User research provides a variety of tools, for examining users' attitudes and behaviors such as usability testing, field research, A/B testing, and analytics.

- **Which creative stakeholders are going to join this process?**

  The people who participate in your design processes and activities play a big role in its structure. Facilitation and coordination of such processes may change to address differences in participants' mental models, expertise, knowledge of the addressed topic, hierarchy in the organization, or existing conflicts. Design processes will, for example, handle the presentation of a context differently if it is addressed to participants coming from the same field compared to those with different backgrounds.

- **Who is going to create the design process?**

  It's not always clear which person or team will propose the new process. There are several aspects that need to be considered in any case: the creators of a process need to have a good understanding of a team's needs, resources, interpersonal relations, communication issues, and interaction with other teams.

  Organizations that ask external teams or individuals to help them create design processes for their creative stakeholders should be aware that an important period of time should be dedicated to providing them with the necessary perspective and information so they can properly understand the challenges, needs, and expectations of the organization and its employees.

  Creative stakeholders, on the other hand, already work and experience the issues in question in their daily work environment and are already aware of the challenges they and their organizations face. So, they could very effectively identify these challenges and potentially define a process to address them themselves. In some cases though, due to office-political reasons, existing conflict or just the fact that it's not always easy to change the way things work, asking for the assistance and support of teams (inside or outside the organization), who might address the situation from an external perspective, might help the creation process move forward faster and more efficiently.

REFLECTION POINTS

Will the process involve experts from the same field, such as a design or development team, or will it involve people with different expertise, such as a joint squad, including user researchers, developers, product managers, and designers?

- In this case, it's possible that not everyone joining the process has the same skills, understanding of the presented problems or context knowledge.
- Is the target audience clear to all participants? Are there any recent or past user research studies that could help participants understand and empathize with users?
- Has your process taken into account participants' understanding of the field? Does the process provide the necessary information for participants to understand the context, available resources, technical limitations, existing solutions, and competition?
- Have the aims of the process or activity been clear to all participants?
- Have you identified the different teams that will need to work together? If yes, will they participate in the process and how? Different configurations and structures will most likely lead to different team dynamics, and hence, the approach that you will need to proceed with may change.

Who is going to work on establishing and revising the process? Is it going to be someone (or everyone) from a team for whom the process is designed, someone outside the team, or someone outside the organization?

5.11 Design Processes Focus on Feasibility and Encourage Innovation

Design processes focus on both feasibility and innovation.

From one side, design processes should help teams to create and perform within their existing circumstances and resources. To achieve this, processes should:

- Offer teams the necessary visibility on the product vision, the tools available, and the technologies and methodologies being used

- Communicate business and organization objectives clearly

- Position customers in the foreground

- Encourage and establish effective communication between team members and different teams inside an organization

- Deal with conflict

- Alleviate any barrier that gets in the way of teams performing and creating

Processes can be used as tools that ensure product and team viability in the foreseeable future, creating the necessary circumstances for deadline-driven delivery, and establishing clarity and common understanding about different teams' goals and the overall shared vision throughout the organization.

At the same time, processes should also encourage innovation by providing creative stakeholders with time and space to engage in creative problem-solving activities; the necessary approaches and tools to scan their environment, continuously examine their customers, challenge existing practices, products, and features, and embrace failure as a natural part of design.

In this way, processes ensure the viability of products and services in the medium and long term. As consumer needs change constantly and rapidly, teams' ability to capture and identify those needs as well as addressing them through new products, services, and features should be encouraged and facilitated through the established design processes.

REFLECTION POINTS

Does your design process address some or all of the following points?

- Offering teams the necessary visibility on:
  - o Product vision
  - o Available tools
  - o Technologies and methodologies being used
- Communicating business and organization objectives clearly
- Providing information about customers, users, and their needs
- Encouraging and establishing effective communication between team members and different teams inside an organization
- Dealing with inter- or intra-team conflict
- Are there any moments, opportunities, or activities during which creative stakeholders can challenge existing tools, process, and knowledge of the addressed topic and explore new solutions?

5.12 Processes Should Incorporate User Research and Help Establish a Collective Memory

Would a ship's captain or airplane pilot embark on a journey without their navigation instruments?

I do hope that your answer was "no"! Ships and planes need compasses, maps, and Global Positioning System (GPS) tracking systems to safely navigate to their destination. Long story short, even if you know where you want to go, you still need the necessary tools to get there. So, why would we do design without research?!

The importance of user research cannot be emphasized enough in the field of design. Without research, design decisions are based on guesses, personal opinions, and our gut instincts. Don't get me wrong, personal experience is really valuable and a very important element for every creative stakeholder. In any case though, we can definitely learn way more by listening to users and observing their actions. A common phenomenon, unfortunately, in the industry is that a reason can always be found not to do research.

Conducting user research also has no value if it is not shared and available to those who need it. It is a great waste of both assets and opportunities when well conducted research stays forgotten in a corner of an organization's intranet, without being known or accessible to everyone in the organization. There are other cases where, even if research has been communicated, its message and content doesn't get through because people cannot handle the cognitive overload of assimilating new information along with the regular tasks of their work process: people receive too many emails, have multiple tasks to deal with, attend several meetings, and may be less motivated to go through report documents, especially if they aren't sure it will have any impact on their work.

That's why design processes should continuously and repetitively integrate user research at various occasions. It's true that there will always be a reason for some stakeholders to postpone or not read research. That's exactly why research should be a fundamental and unavoidable component of the design process. Processes should be able to not only provide visibility on research affecting a team's work but also inform people about other teams' work. In this way, a global vision, cohesion, and shared understanding of the challenges and problems of different areas in the organization are shared and known. Design processes, being intrinsically motivating, should make sure that the way that research is delivered and presented should be fun, interesting, and easy to process.

Design processes should make sure that the way that research is delivered and presented should be fun, interesting, and easy to process.

Last but not least, design processes that manage to promote and diffuse knowledge coming from user research eventually help establish a collective memory among creative stakeholders. This collective memory is based on:

- Best practices
- Previously faced challenges
- Known successes and failures

I have noticed that on many occasions, there are one or two people in the organization that know the history of the product they are working on (usually these people had worked on the project from the beginning), giving examples of what worked well, what challenges the teams faced, and why certain decisions were taken at a given time.

REFLECTION POINTS

Does your process diffuse user research to different creative stakeholders?

- Is your process supported by user researchers in the organization? If yes, do they participate in the process and when?
- At what points of your process is research taken into account?
- Does your process encourage creative stakeholders to go through existing or previous studies?
- Is previous research accessible? If yes, are credentials and repositories available to all members of the process?
- Creative stakeholders may be overwhelmed by too much information. Are there any activities, approaches, or tools for presenting the most important takeaways of different user research?
- Testing with real users is crucial for effective and efficient design. Does your process encourage testing with real users?

It's great that at least someone knows these things, but it would be even greater if that information was common knowledge for everyone in the team. That's why design processes should be able to diffuse information, educate, and continuously keep creative stakeholders informed about the past, the present, and the future, making them more effective at doing what they do.

5.13 Processes Break Silos and Encourage Co-creation

Whether we want to or not, on some occasions we get overfocused on our own tasks and field of expertise. This is normal when we consider how, as we grow older, we develop specific mental models that make us better at processing information related to the fields that we put more emphasis on. As a result, we read more about our own field, we hang out with people from our field, and we pay more attention to studies and outcomes at work which are related to our specialty.

Additionally, there are several reasons why teams and individuals may communicate more (or less) with others. Organizational structure, office politics, team dynamics, unresolved conflict, and available resources such as time, team size, intranet messaging tools, or management decisions may cause lack of communication, weak interaction, and exchange of information and minimum collaboration (sometimes the atmosphere may even get competitive and counterproductive) between different teams and individual creative stakeholders. In some cases, the atmosphere may even get competitive and counterproductive between different teams and individual creative stakeholders.

These invisible walls that we build have an impact both on us and the products that we work on.

Design processes should break down these walls, establishing proactive and fruitful relationships between individuals and teams, with the goal of eventually creating an atmosphere full of positive energy and shared values united behind a common vision. Design processes are about co-creating. In other words, the final outcome is the result of the joint effort of several actors, who communicate, share problems, expectations, and outcomes, leading to teams that grow and evolve together.

REFLECTION POINTS

Do you know what types of creative stakeholders are participating in your design process?

It's possible that stakeholders coming from different backgrounds don't necessarily understand other participants' fields, interests, and way of working. Do you intend to organize any activities so that different stakeholders can introduce themselves and their fields of expertise?

Does your process encourage the participation of different experts in the proposed activities? Problem finding and problem solving become way more effective when experts from different fields add their perspectives.

Are teams in the organization aware of other teams' work?

Does your process communicate teams' work to the organization?

- What have been the successes of teams involved in the process?
- What things did the teams learn during this process?
- Are there repositories with information that can be made available to different members of the organization?

5.14 Processes Focus on Short- and Long-Term Outcomes and Have Different Durations

For every design problem, there is a design process that can be put in place. This also means that design processes, depending on what we need them for, may have a different duration and expected outcomes.

There are, for instance, design processes that focus on long-term outcomes, such as:

- Establishing a general workflow for a design team or the interaction of design teams with other teams in the organization, such as development, marketing, QA, product, and so on.

- Proposing a UX strategy for a product or set of products.

- Improving communication between creative stakeholders inside and outside teams.

- Reinforcing human-centricity in the design process.

In the scope of our analysis, we will consider long-term processes as those whose application duration is long or whose outcomes become tangible after some time has passed. As a result, applying them may take a while to be noticed. Consequently, the outcomes and the long-term aspect of the process need to be clearly presented and understood by the impacted teams as well as management. Long-term processes are also iterative. This means that even if we aim for outcomes that will be visible in the medium or long term, corrective actions leading to process change will most likely also be taken based on user research, team feedback, and market or technology developments occurring in the early stages of adopting and applying such processes.

There are also design processes that focus on short-term outcomes, such as:

- Coming up with design ideas for an upcoming product, such as the process to formulate designs for a minimum viable product.

- Brainstorming and proposing solutions for design problems.

- Addressing technical malfunctions or bugs that disrupt the normal use of websites and platforms.

- Setting an initial direction for the design of a product or service.

It is very possible that processes with long-term outcomes incorporate processes or activities that are aiming at short-term outcomes. We have already looked at the connection between processes and activities and how they are interconnected. There are processes that may consist of several activities and there are several activities that are based on processes. In the same way, processes with short-term outcomes may be driven by broader design processes and, inversely, processes with long-term goals may need to apply processes whose outcomes will be tangible in the short term.

In both cases, design processes can have many forms, from very abstract guidelines and sets of steps to concrete workshops. The form and structure of design processes are also affected by the duration we want and expect it to have. Duration can span from a few minutes to a few years, depending on the aims of each individual design process. It may also be impacted by the number of steps and phases that need to be covered per activity or process or, as we previously called it, granularity. There are several factors that affect the duration of activities. For that reason, there will be a dedicated chapter on group dynamics later on, where we will examine how to estimate and propose the optimal duration for the sessions you want to build.

5.15 Processes Take into Account Organizational Complexity but Don't Reinforce It

In an ideal world, design processes should be detached from the bad habits of existing organizational structures. Organizational complexity can easily stifle innovation, impede communication, and negatively impact final products. Design processes should work to alleviate those issues and not exacerbate them.

Drafting design processes based on existing methods and practices that are the very reasons why a design process is needed in the first place is definitely not a good idea. Instead, issues concerning methods, practices, communication gaps, misalignments between teams, and interconnection between different departments and teams should be mapped in advance so that they can be improved through the proposed design processes. Design processes can then be adapted to address design problems, establish communication between teams that couldn't communicate before, and create a shared understanding and direction of a product vision.

Another aspect to consider is that design processes are adopted by organizations when stakeholders understand their value and they subsequently get management support. Hence, it is only then that they are effective. Part of establishing a design process requires getting buy-in from management as well as displaying, throughout the organization, how a specific process could improve people's work lives and output. As a result, the impact of establishing and applying a design process should not only be communicated and made visible to the teams involved in the design process but also to the organization, explaining aspects where the process has actually brought value to the organization and its members.

Explain how a new process will bring value to the organization

Instead of simply presenting the process itself

REFLECTION POINTS

Have you identified any organizational structures that cause communication issues, misalignments between teams, or conflicts within or between teams? If yes, how does your process address them?

Have you identified the benefits of applying your process? Do you have existing data to back up your points? If not, do you have arguments, and potentially a presentation, to explain your process's value to other stakeholders?

5.16 Design Processes Improve the Efficiency of Already Established Processes

In many cases, design processes need to be applied on top of previously established organizational processes. These processes may be focused on specific teams or broader organizational workflows. A very good example is Agile frameworks, which are continuously adopted by all types of companies, from the small to the very large. On several occasions, design processes are introduced to organizations that may be already working with a specific framework, presenting limitations and opportunities.

A common concern when new design processes are proposed is whether or not they will impact or invalidate what already exists. This is also one of the main hesitations of management when it comes to moving forward with such initiatives. This argument is valid: design processes shouldn't be introduced as a "Big Bang explosion" that changes the world as we know it and demands changes of cataclysmic proportions for "the greater good."

Instead, design processes can identify the points where existing processes fail or underperform and address them through new proactive measures. On top of this, before starting work on a new design process, it would be good to examine the pros and cons of previously established processes, learning from them, and forming your new design process on the wisdom that you have drawn.

REFLECTION POINTS

Are there previously established processes in the organization that are impacting design?

- What are the strong aspects of those processes?
- What are the week aspects of those processes?
- How could these processes be improved?
- Would a separate design process help teams or the organization to be more efficient? It is possible that by improving existing broader processes, team efficiency may already improve.
- Are there particularities related to design that need to be taken into account either through the existing or a new process? For example:
  - o It is possible that designers may need to work on designing some sprints before their implementation.
  - o Usability tests may be required before going into the development phase, which requires some time to prepare.
  - o Some design teams ask for feedback from stake-holders, coming from fields such as management, marketing, development, and reiterate before moving to the development phase.
  - o After designs have been developed and released, it's possible that usability testing and analytics may point out usability issues and opportunities for improve-ment. Time to reiterate and improve those designs may be needed.
- How can your potential new design process be aligned with existing processes? Are there any dependencies? It is possible that these processes may have common/shared phases or steps?

5.17 Processes Present Mitigation Strategies

Since not all processes are the same, there is a considerable pos-sibility that design teams may be presented with situations where not all the steps or phases of existing and popular processes may be applicable. For example, for a company or product that lacks analytics, how would a design process account for the lack of insights and user behavior? What mitigation actions could it propose in order to help design teams come up with informed decisions?

Consequently, effective identification of the shortcomings and weaknesses of any process can help design teams anticipate potential issues and propose actions that may mitigate deviations, problems, and challenges.

REFLECTION POINTS

Are there any weaknesses or potential issues that have been identified throughout your process?
    Are there any mitigation actions that address those issues? Who is involved in those actions?

5.18 Representation and Form

The way that we represent design processes has a great impact on how creative stakeholders perceive and use them. As we saw previously, there is a diverse set of existing design processes, which are presented in different ways and forms. Some follow straight lines (with either horizontal or vertical element arrangements), while others are represented through circles.

Even though the arrangement of process steps and phases may not be a big deal for their creators, they really make a difference to how others will understand them. It's important to consider that not all stakeholders will pay the same attention or invest the same energy in the application and set-up of a design process. Hence, an incorrect understanding on their part may impact the adoption, application, and overall future of design processes.

There are several aspects that can be taken into account when representing one's process, including:

5.18.1 Straight Lines versus Circles and Loops

Processes can be represented in straight lines and they may be either horizontal, like this:

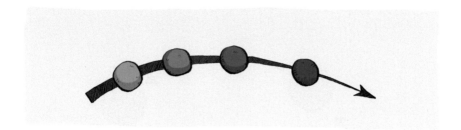

or vertical, like this:

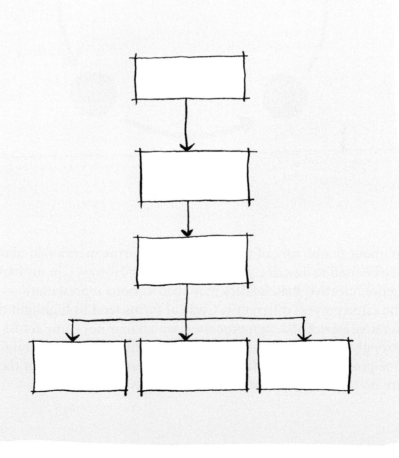

Design processes may also be represented in cyclical or other loop forms, like these:

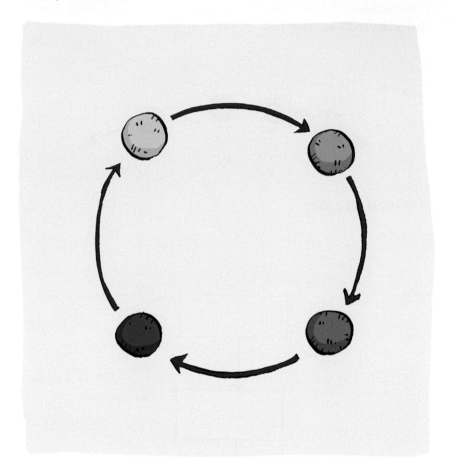

Without doubt, any of the presentation forms mentioned above can be used to describe yourdesign process. However, in my experience, creative stakeholders may read various representations of the same process differently. Cyclical forms tend to highlight the iterative aspect of design processes, which may not come across as strongly in straight lines, for instance. On the other hand, straight-line process representations tend to be easier to read when there are many phases and steps, compared to cyclical formats.

5.18.2 Linearity versus Nonlinearity

As we have seen, there are processes that are based on a specific sequence of steps while there are others that are set up around a nonlinear format, where some steps may not be necessary for their completion or that going back to previous steps may be necessary in order to advance further.

In any of these cases, this linear or nonlinear nature needs to be presented to creative stakeholders in order to remove potential ambiguity on the application and use of that process by a team or organization

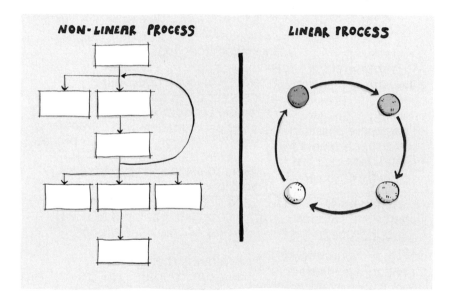

Who is your audience?

Who are the people impacted by your process?

How many people are impacted by your process?

Does your process encourage conducting, consulting and communication on user research?

Does your process provide opportunities for analytical or synthetical thinking?

Do creative stakeholders have the opportunity to identify new problems or re-frame existing ones?

Will it be a broad process, an activity or a set of activities?

Is your process linear or non-linear?

How much does your process focus on a part of a broader system? How much does your process focus on conveying the whole product vision to its participants?

How granular is your process?

Are there phases or steps that are optional and ones that are indispensable?

How scalable and adaptable is your process to potential team and organizational structure changes? Can it be used in other teams of the organization?

What are the phases and steps of your process?

Does your process encourage innovation? Does your process examine ideas for their feasibility?

What is the duration of your process?

Does your process encourage communication and synergies with other teams?

Chapter 6

The Process Core

DOI: 10.1201/9781003050445-7

6.1 Five Important Questions

Some years ago, my team had organized a set of meetings, aimed at helping us design an upcoming project. We went to each meeting with great excitement, holding our colorful sticky notes and our fat markers, and we came up with ideas which we later discussed. After a couple of meetings however, we noticed something peculiar: we had started meandering and going around in circles. The meetings were getting longer and longer, and our patience was running thin.

It was not until a colleague raised her hand and said "Excuse me, but are we sure we're all talking about the same customers?" that we figured out what was going on: we were not aligned from the very beginning on the scope of the activities we were doing. Even if we were physically co-located and had been presented with the same information about the scope of the project, our customers, and our resources during the first meeting, people had processed this information from their own perspective, creating as many interpretations of the problem as there were participants in the room. As a result, all the activities that followed depicted everyone's fuzzy understanding of the problems we had to solve and their components.

The fact that people are physically located in the same room, reading or listening to the same information doesn't mean that they have the same understanding of an activity and the problem it aims to solve.

So, before trying to come up with stunning designs that mesmerize your audience, during your own sessions make sure that:

All people participating in your processes and activities have understood the problems to be addressed and their components.

Design processes exist to make sure of this. Consequently, they should be able to help creative stakeholders respond to five important questions. Let's check them all one by one:

6.1.1 Who does your team consist of?

There are no solutions to problems without problem solvers. Sometimes we tend to focus so much on problems themselves that we forget that **creative stakeholders are the main problem-solving power in any design process.**

Design teams consist of creative stakeholders who are different in terms of personality, temperament, communication skills, knowledge, and competency level as well as their overall field of expertise. Like a chemical experiment, this potent mix of diversity can be a powerful weapon for coming up with innovative solutions, where different minds contribute to forging new and successful outcomes for the team and product. However, it can also turn into a time bomb if not managed and handled properly.

I have encountered several situations where projects have gone south just because stakeholders couldn't properly collaborate and co-create. There are several reasons that can lead to such an outcome, such as:

- Poor communication
- Difference of opinions
- Lack of leadership
- Lack of colocation
- Character differences

On the other hand, I have joined amazing and well-established teams, where the existing design process (or lack of design process) would render design boring, dull, and unmotivating. I can promise you that the end results for all those cases would be much better if the processes made design more interesting and exciting.

We already saw that successful design processes are intrinsically motivating, creating experiences during which we design while having fun. Since we are all so unique in how we perceive and interact with the world around us, design processes need to take into account our unique nature and facilitate experiences where we communicate with our peers and become a team.

The first step towards building teams is through identifying and clarifying who will be affected by the envisioned design process and how. There are several ways to approach this question, two of which are getting to know creative stakeholders as individuals and as field experts:

When **we examine creative stakeholders as individuals**, we try to understand their professional and personal needs, expectations, soft skills, and ways that they interact and communicate with others. In this way, we can identify what's important for them, address problems they face about interactions with their peers and management, focus their strong competences, and use them to the team's advantage and see how the lack of a certain skill can be addressed in the broader scope of a team and process.

Examining creative stakeholders as field experts, on the other hand, can help us identify each of their technical skills as well as their interaction and position in the organization. It's important to remember that design processes may be proposed for people who are not necessarily members of the same team. For instance, a design process may affect a designer, a developer, a user researcher, and a product manager who work on a dedicated project but each of whom may be members of dedicated design, development, research, and product teams, respectively. As a result, by examining creative stakeholders as field experts, we can better understand how different teams may be impacted and what channels and measures may be needed in order to ensure good communication and visibility between all members participating in a design process.

6.1.2 Who is your audience?

Products and services are conceived for a target audience of customers and users. Customers and users are not necessarily the same thing since the people who buy our products are not necessarily the ones who will be using them. A typical example are large organizations, where special dedicated departments are tasked with buying software solution packages, which will later be used by other teams. There are of course multiple cases where customers and users are the same people. For instance, people who purchase apps on their mobile phones for their own use are both customers and users.

Whether your products are mobile apps, business-to-business (B2B) portals, dashboards, Learning Management Systems (LMS), or video games, they aim at addressing particular user needs. Hence, they offer some kind of value to how users work, communicate, and live. Products that fail to propose real value, sooner or later, perish. This is actually very common; we quite often see, for instance, organizations or teams trying to figure out ways to push the technologies they have come up with to their audience, leading to fancy products that eventually gain very little traction. This is not because the teams behind those technologies were not skilled enough; it's because these products were not conceived based on actual human needs.

Customers and users have their own needs and expectations of the products they use. They use them because they want their needs fulfilled. These needs may be related to entertainment, communication, efficiency, task fulfillment, transportation, education, and so on. Being able to identify these needs and expectations helps teams drive their designs towards specific directions that have meaning for their audiences. These needs and expectations may be clearly stated by users or may be identified by design teams, after conducting user research.

Since we are all unique, we all interact with technology differently and show individual attitudes towards products and services. We have our rituals, we organize our workplace differently than others, and, when presented with new technologies, we interact with them in different ways and at various paces. This is because, during our lives, we learn and process information around us uniquely, constructing knowledge in our own manner. As a result, we all build our own mental models, which help us interpret and understand the world around us. Users have their own mental models. Even if these mental models are unique, on many occasions, there are portions of our broader audience that share common attributes. In that way, we can potentially segment and better coordinate our design strategies.

6.1.3 What are your business objectives?

Every organization, from startups to large corporations, has its own missions and objectives. Whether these objectives are profit related or nonprofit related, often their viability and sustainability rely on those objectives. Startups, game studios, and large corporations, for instance, need to produce profit to ensure the continuity of their operations, while nongovernment organizations or educational institutions are tasked with targets they need to accomplish that have social rather than monetary outcomes.

In any case, knowing these business objectives gives us a point of reference in a world with infinite design possibilities. By knowing the business objectives of our organization, we can find design solutions that help the organization to achieve them. For those of you thinking of our previous discussions around user-centricity, accomplishing business objectives and being user-centered aren't mutually exclusive notions! Being user-centered is still our goal!

In fact, **the experiences that we create need to be both user-centered and business-facilitating**. In other words, our designs need to fulfill both the needs of our users and the organizations that create them. Whether we realize it or not, these two aspects are very well linked from the beginning anyway: creating products and services that are indeed welcomed and used by customers requires them to provide some type of value. So, creating user-centered experiences, which will be adopted and used by our users, is the basis for the achievement of their own goals and missions.

There are several ways to describe and define objectives, one of which is the SMART objectives criteria [16]. SMART is an acronym, standing for the following criteria:

- **Simple**: We already said that simplicity is gold! Simple objectives are easy to express, clarify fuzziness, and provide us with a good opportunity to better structure our thoughts and remove unneeded clutter, as objectives may often not be initially clear even for us.

- **Measurable**: By being able to measure progress towards the accomplishment of objectives, design teams can track whether or not they have completely or partially achieved them.

- **Assignable**: Being able to assign responsibility for who will work on and accomplish specific objectives can help teams to better organize themselves, identify ownership, and improve communication.

- **Realistic**: Even if being ambitious often helps push teams forward, objectives need to be realistic, so that they can eventually be accomplished within a team's particular context and resources.

- **Time-bound**: If something can be achieved 'anytime' then it lacks focus and measurement loses value. Identifying a cutoff point in advance helps teams identify and prioritize goals.

There are several variations for the notions included in SMART around the industry and international bibliography. Pick the one that you think best addresses your team's needs. In any case, the main advantage of knowing your business objectives is that from now on you will have a point of reference when making your decisions, since they will need to address both user and business needs.

6.1.4 What is the domain context you are going to be working in?

Let's start by picturing an umbrella. For some, an umbrella is a tool we use on rainy days, an item associated with moody weather, wind, and preferring not to be outdoors. We could also, however, imagine placing an umbrella on a sunny beach. Now the whole mental picture has shifted: we now think of sandy beaches, perfect weather, beach tennis, and diving into a warm sea. The only thing that changed between those two paradigms is context. And context changes everything!

Problems acquire meaning inside the context through which we examine them. Problems may be defined and understood differently and, consequently, solutions may vary from case to case and from context to context. Context encompasses several aspects, including the industry and the field we are working in, our audience and their habits, and the broader environment and world we live in.

Coming up with solutions without first examining the competition and what has previously been accomplished in your field is like trying to reinvent the wheel. In fact, it's even worse, since teams may invest resources into solutions that might already exist or have been proposed and failed. As a result, being able to see how one's field works and has evolved, including both successes and failures, offers teams valuable insights and may help them save valuable resources. Last but not least, being able to understand one's competitors, as well as their strengths and weaknesses provides teams with the opportunity to reflect upon potential opportunities for the problems they are asked to solve.

Context is also defined by culture, which is a notion that encompasses many aspects of our lives, whether we realize it or not. Cultures are shared standards and ways of behavior that we develop when we interact with others. There are cultures related to food, dress codes, digital habits, and communication. The list never ends. Players of Massive Multiplayer Online games for instance develop their own codes of conduct, use special jargon, and develop habits that feel bizarre for people who aren't part of their culture but which have a special meaning for them. Understanding the characteristics of the cultures we are targeting gives us insights on habits, trends, fears, and expectations which can help us better define our audiences but also identify and solve problems that have meaning for them.

Being able to scan and monitor the world around us can be a source of great incentive and inspiration. Whether it's obvious or not, general socioeconomic events may have a direct or indirect impact on our products, our audiences, and ourselves, requiring corrective actions and potential redefinition and reframing of the problems we started off solving. Economic recessions or developments, scientific discoveries, engineering breakthroughs, development, or collapse of other fields and sectors, which are seemingly unrelated to the one we are designing for, could potentially give birth to new design problems, and hence new opportunities, which we could solve.

6.1.5 What are your resources?

Not all teams have the same resources. There are teams that have big budgets, numerous members, existing know-how, time, and necessary tools and there are teams that don't. However, we very often see amazing results from teams with limited numbers of people and resources. This is because these teams optimized their process and adapted to their available resources.

Resources can be related to several aspects of design, including (but not limited to) budget, team size, team expertise, time, available tools, or access to external support. Another important aspect regarding resources are legacy artifacts, which describe any pre-existing tools, resources, designs, or code that teams need to work with. Especially, when working on existing platforms, teams need to improve existing designs and codes implemented on technical stacks which seem like the best idea at the moment of their inception but may later on become obsolete or pose restrictions to the solutions that teams want to propose. Knowing them before starting to work on one's process helps teams anticipate and better adapt their solutions to their available resources.

Consequently, an abundance of resources means very little if we can't make the most of them. In order to properly and efficiently use them however would require knowing what resources we have at our disposal in the first place.

6.1.6 Onsite and Remote Work Configurations

Physical proximity and remote work can play a great role in setting up one's design process. Design processes need to take into account how team members interact and communicate and try to address and facilitate potential issues that may arise from the existing location configuration. The Covid-19 pandemic has been a very good example of this aspect, since it imposed on several occasions remote working conditions for individuals and teams.

Teams that are based on a remote configuration or hybrid configurations for instance need tools that facilitate communication, the exchange of information, and resource sharing. Hence, a design process would need to take into account the existence of video-conferencing tools, instant messaging services, and shared resource repositories and try to address potential issues that may arise from the participation (or lack of participation) from different stakeholders, making sure that all team members have enough visibility on the product vision and the project aspects that concern them.

On the other hand, there are several examples of teams that are based onsite and still have considerable communication issues. Physical proximity, desk placement, and personal and team dynamics are just some of the factors that may affect onsite communication, which could be addressed by design processes in this context.

Another common configuration of teams, especially encountered in large corporations, is a mix of remote and onsite work, where entire teams are based at one location and need to collaborate with other teams who are physically located somewhere else. Even if all stakeholders are physically located at a company office, there may still be considerable physical distance between creative stakeholders, who may need to establish a process that accounts for that particular hybrid configuration.

6.2 The Process Core

If we were to imagine processes as well-oiled design machines, the five questions that we previously examined would be their gears.

- Knowing the members of our teams helps us to figure out our team's strengths and weaknesses, allowing us to build processes that take advantage of both of them.

- By knowing our audience and our business objectives, we have a design compass that can guide us through the amazing journey that our teams embark on. We can explore solutions that address our users' needs and help our organization achieve its missions.

- Understanding the context around which we are asked to solve problems helps us identify and suggest ways to solve them, making our proposals relevant. We perform better if we know what we can and cannot do in the circumstances we work under and the resources we have.

At any point, design processes should be able to respond to these five questions. These five questions are indeed so important that we could think of them like the heart of a design process, or perhaps… a core!

This core places creative stakeholders at the "center of the universe," since they are tasked with the very important mission of finding and solving problems through design. Creative stakeholders analyze and understand their audience, business needs, and the context in which they are asked to work and, through optimizing the resources that they possess, perform, and create meaningful experiences for their customers and users.

Eventually, all these elements are materialized into a continuous, iterative problem-finding and problem-solving flow, which always gives and receives feedback to and from the core, leading to activities that are meaningful and fun for creative stakeholders and have value for customers, users, and organizations.

REFLECTION POINTS 🔍

Your Participants

- What is your participants' expertise?
- Are your participant members of the same or different teams? If they come from different teams, what are the dependencies and relationships between those teams? Are there any communication actions that could ameliorate the inter-team communication?
- Where are your participants located? Is the team co-located? Are some or all members located remotely? How does proximity, different time zones, and the need for synchronization affect the process you want to create and how could potential issues be addressed?
- Are there any personal or professional preferences and needs regarding tools, ways of working, or communication inside and outside their teams?
- Are there any aspects related to creative stakeholders' relations that you need to take into account when designing your process? Are there any organizational particularities, political issues, or interpersonal relations that could positively or negatively affect the established process?

Your Audience

- Have you conducted user research on your target audience?
- Are you aware of demographic characteristics that define your audience?
- Are you aware of behaviors or attitudes of your audience regarding the products or services you intend to design?
- Are there any particular audience needs and expectations regarding the products and services you want to design?
- Have you conducted user research on your target audience?

Your Business Objectives

- Are your business objectives Simple, Measurable, Assignable, Realistic, Time-bound?

Your Context

- Are there existing studies regarding the audience in your context?
- Are there existing studies regarding the market, industry, and challenges of this field?
- Have you performed environmental scanning, including economic recessions or developments that may affect the market, scientific discoveries, engineering break-throughs, or growth or collapse of other fields that may impact the products or services that you wish to design?
- Have you researched your competition? What are their strengths and weaknesses?

Your Resources

- Do you have visibility on your project's budget?
- Do you know your team's size?
- What types of experts does your team consist of?
- Are there any tools (design systems, design tools, repos-itories, etc.) that your team needs for this process?
- Can your team request support from other teams? If yes, which teams are they and who are the people to contact?
- Are there any legacy artifacts that you need to take into account?
- Is there physical distance between team members?

  - Are all team members working remotely or is there a portion of the team that works remotely and another one that works onsite?
  - Are there any mitigation actions that will establish visibility of individual and team work throughout the team, in the case of a remote or hybrid location team configuration?
  - Are all team members working remotely? If yes, are there any special provisions to facilitate and improve their work environment under those circumstances? Are necessary tools, activities, or steps already in place? If not, what tools, activities, or steps could be introduced?

Chapter 7

Don't Force It, Play!

DOI: 10.1201/9781003050445-8

7.1 Play Is a Serious Matter

In an experiment conducted by George Land and Beth Jarman [17], a paper clip was presented to a thousand students, who were asked to propose ways of using it. The researchers performed the experiment on the same students at three different moments: when they were 5, 10, and 15 years old. Students who would provide a certain minimum number of answers to the paperclip question were considered as "divergent thinking geniuses." The analysis of the results showed that at the age of 5, 98% of students were ranked at the genius level. The astonishing observation though is that only 12% of the same students could provide the sufficient number of proposals to be considered as a genius at the age of 15.

As it turns out, **creativity can be unlearned** or, in other words, **uncreative ways of thinking can be learned!**

Even if there are definitely several reasons behind this phenomenon, I want to emphasize two that are very relevant to design:

- **Reason #1—Fear of failure:** One of the greatest setbacks in design processes is demonizing failure. When they are afraid of being criticized or looked down upon, creative stakeholders may limit their focus around solutions that are safe, barely building upon what's already known, if at all. Eventually, they may suppress or not express other ideas that cause them to be criticized and then "look bad." This phenomenon drives head-on against the very nature of creativity and innovation, since both of these notions are based on an exploratory and inquisitive approach, where failure is not a side-effect but a natural component of the problem-solving process.

- **Reason #2—Detaching play from design:** We always work best when our heart is set on the tasks we want to achieve. Teams and organizations sometimes tend to forget that the most important element of design is the creative stakeholders: when they are happy, teams perform well, providing value both for users and their organizations. When creative stakeholders are frustrated, confused, bored, and unmotivated, teams underperform. Therefore, understanding what creative stakeholders need is part of creating efficient design processes. Processes that are interesting, encourage us to be creative, give us some freedom, allow us to contribute, help us evolve, indulge our curiosity, and, most importantly, they allow us to play.

I am sure that some people may find play outside the scope of the corporate world. **They are simply and utterly mistaken**. For some people play is only related to toys, video games, and kids' activities; however, play is an indispensable and fundamental component of every human activity. We can perform any action in a playful or a nonplayful manner, from mopping the floor to facilitating ideation workshops. As a result, we can be playful and still be professional. More importantly, when we play, we are not afraid of failing, as failure is part of play.

So, if play is an expression of every human behavior, what we should try to figure isn't whether or not we should integrate it into our design processes but, instead, how we can get the most out of it. Even more, we should be trying to find out how we can transform our design processes into intrinsically motivating experiences for our creative stakeholders. Facilitating play definitely helps on that front.

There are always people who are skeptical about using play in the work environment. This is because they make a mental link between play and chaos and wasted time. If this was actually the case, then they'd have a point. However, **play doesn't mean chaos**. In fact, being able to facilitate playful activities requires serious thought, work, and preparation. Most importantly, it requires a good understanding of how people think and feel as well as the characteristics of play.

In this chapter, we will examine different attributes of play and how it can emerge as a fundamental element of any design process. The objective of reading this chapter is not to create design games, even though that's a possibility, but rather to propose design processes that facilitate and encourage playful activities that are appropriate and pertinent for the contexts and teams you want to address.

7.2 Design Processes Should Be Intrinsically Motivating

Let's start by stating the obvious: **Not all projects and tasks we work on are interesting.**

Some of them challenge our skills and way of thinking, present us with contexts that we didn't know before, the exploration of which excites us and makes us want to know more. Such projects help us learn and evolve, not only as professionals but also as individuals. They also help us fulfill some of our personal desires and needs. Other projects, however, get associated with dull or unpleasant moments, during which we engage in activities we don't enjoy, repeat the same boring steps again and again, get trapped in situations that we'd prefer to avoid, and eventually make us want to leave the team or organization.

We tend to perform better when we engage in tasks that we enjoy and feel happy working on. In cases like this, we are more focused on the tasks at hand, sometimes we even forget to eat while working on them, we keep thinking about them, and we want to dig through them more even after work. This is because these tasks have intrinsic value for us. Such types of experiences give our work some purpose, address our needs, and give us fulfillment. Consequently, they are motivating for us. Motivation can be identified in two categories:

1. **Intrinsic motivation**, which describes personal and internal desires and needs. Intrinsic motivation is the result of our inherent interest in particular activities and tasks themselves. People who find pleasure in drawing, for instance, will likely develop their drawing skills more than people who don't, as they'll be invested in the activity whether someone asks them to be or not. Activities that are intrinsically motivating hold a special value for us, as they are not associated with external rewards, such as money, fame, or recognition.

2. **Extrinsic motivation**, which is related to actions we take based on external stimuli or situations, such as rewards

or punishment. Extrinsic motivation is based on the idea that some states, elements, or activities can motivate us to engage in specific activities. A work bonus is an example of extrinsic motivation: employees may pay more effort to achieving their work objectives in order to get their bonus, which potentially they wouldn't otherwise.

INTRINSIC MOTIVATION

EXTRINSIC MOTIVATION

Successful design processes are intrinsically motivating, since they manage to present intrinsic value and meaning for creative stakeholders. However, not all activities present the same intrinsic value for all creative stakeholders. As we are all unique, intrinsically motivating activities differ from person to person and from team to team.

7.3 So, What Is Play?

Play is not easy to define because, as a notion, it is connected with almost everything we do. Swiss psychologist Jean Piaget characterized play as an aspect or expression of any human activity [18].

As a result, every activity can be performed in a playful or a nonplayful manner [19,20]. There is a difference, for instance, between participating in a meeting where we simply listen and participating in the same meeting while listening and drafting doodles based on discussion topics that catch our attention. Similarly, there is a difference between introducing different meeting participants by just stating their names and introducing the same participants by stating their names and their favorite childhood meal.

The question that is raised then is how can we consider that an action is playful or not? In fact, play is based on the balance between different elements, which it consists of. So, let's examine some of those elements:

- **Play is autotelic**. Autotelic means that the very aim of joining an activity is the activity itself. This is the case with play: we decide to join playful activities because they are themselves interesting. When people force us to participate in an activity, it's not play anymore. An autotelic activity needs to present an intrinsic value for people. For instance, developers that like solving complex and elaborate algorithmic problems will find participating in a hackathon interesting and meaningful in itself. They mightn't be participating because a manager told them to but just because they want to.

- **Play is pleasure.** One of the biggest reasons why people play is because play is fun! However, not all fun activities are connected with play. Enjoying a cold mojito on a sun lounger or hanging out with friends may be fun, but we wouldn't normally associate them with play. However, the activities we just looked at acquire another, more playful, meaning if we exercise some effort: Exploring the ingredients of a mojito and trying to create a new cocktail or trying to dress your friends in the most ridiculous outfits we can find. A key characteristic of play is that people have the ability to put effort into activities that they enjoy, leading to pleasure.

- **Play is about surprises.** Game designer Jesse Schell [19] considers play fun because it includes pleasure and surprises. This means that in play there is always something at stake: How many slam dunks can you achieve in 5 minutes? Will you manage to remember all the names of everyone at a meeting? Will you be able to solve the given puzzle? There are of course cases, where unorganized activities can be playful. Doodling is a good example, since we often don't know what the shapes we draw actually correspond to, providing an element of surprise. The element of uncertainty provides an interesting perspective for the notion of play.

- **Play facilitates flow.** Flow is a state of mind characterized by intense focus and pleasure, where people are immersed in a task that is intrinsically motivating [21]. People achieve the flow state when they participate in activities that are balanced, helping them avoid boredom, anxiety, or frustration. Psychologist Mihalyi Csíkszentmihályi considered that the challenge of the activities we participate in when we play should be matched by a necessary set of skills. When we play a new game, for instance, we have no particular skills at that game. So, the levels we start out on are easy. As the difficulty becomes greater and the challenge increases, players get anxious. Players who continue playing, and don't go back to easier levels, develop the necessary skills to match the level difficulty, achieving balance between their skillset and the presented challenges. If they stay at the same, easy, level of challenge for a while, even after having developed the necessary competences to advance, they get bored. Hence, the game needs to become more challenging as our skills develop. As a result, when we play, we always search for an equilibrium between anxiety and boredom, which looks like this:

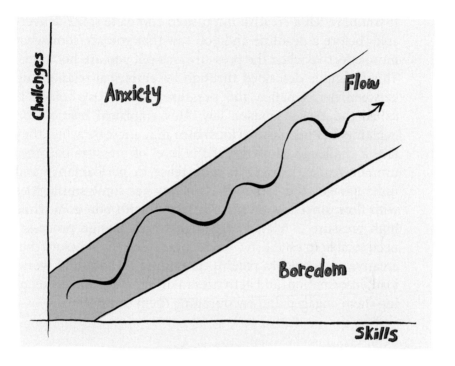

Flow is very relevant in design processes. One of the dynamics that processes try to balance is challenge versus boredom. When we join new teams and processes, we need the necessary information, skills, and competences to deal with the particular challenges of organizations, teams, and projects. As a result, we gradually take on more challenging tasks as we develop our understanding and develop our competences for the situations that we face. When the challenge is enormous for the skills we possess, we may feel overwhelmed, anxious, or frustrated. When we aren't challenged enough, on the other hand, we get bored. Consequently, design processes need to be able to address the way that different people and teams evolve and grow within the organization and adapt the level of challenge for their existing skills.

- **Play can be a bit stressful but not too much**. Even if too much stress can have negative effects on people, some pressure may potentially make people more efficient at performing tasks. If you have felt a creative impulse to complete some deliverables before a deadline and you saw that you are somewhat more effective when the pressure was on, you are not alone. This feeling is described through an empirical relationship between performance and pressure that in psychology is called the Yerkes-Dodson law. This empirical relationship explains that people's performance may increase when they face a challenge. However, if the level of pressure becomes unmanageable, it leads to a decrease in performance and unhappiness. The Yerkes-Dodson law has some similarities with flow, since low pressure is related with boredom while high pressure is related with high stress. Design processes need to able to establish a balance between the pressure that creative stakeholders receive, providing the optimal workload, information, and activities in different instances, keeping them engaged and encouraging them to perform.

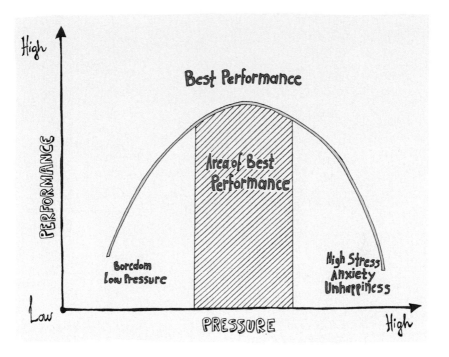

Chapter **8**

An Introduction to Team Dynamics

DOI: 10.1201/9781003050445-9

If some of your experiences working in a team have stunk, you're not alone!

Since working with team members accounts for a considerable portion of our professional (and sometimes personal) lives, **being part of teams we love and feel comfortable in is more than just important**: in fact it's indispensable for our performance, our happiness, and the existence of the organizations we're part of.

Creating teams that work efficiently and harmoniously isn't anything like shooting fish in a barrel, however. In fact, building teams is both challenging and complex as it requires working with one of the most unfathomable things in the universe: human nature.

As we already saw, design processes and activities may last from a few minutes to several months or years. The way that teams are formed will also vary from context to context. For a team of stakeholders, for instance, who don't know each other, getting together for a 2-hour ideation workshop will have different team dynamics and needs than an existing team that wants to build a design process for their daily workflow.

In this chapter, we are going to explore different factors that positively contribute to the creation of happy and efficient design teams.

8.1 Teams Are Built, Not Designated

Team building is like baking a cake: you may have all the necessary high-quality ingredients to mix together, but you need to bake them in order to have a fluffy and delicious cake.

The fact that we are placed in teams doesn't necessarily mean that we can all co-exist and co-create.

No matter how talented the creative stakeholders are, team building requires that they get to know and understand each other and, eventually, find a configuration and process that helps them achieve both their common and individual goals. Getting to know and understand each other is not always that straightforward, however.

We are all so different, carrying our own idiosyncrasies, experiences, and perspectives of the world as well as our own personal and professional problems. We have different temperaments and priorities and we react to pressure or conflict in disparate ways. All in all, there are moments when we can't even understand ourselves, let alone our colleagues.

Let's imagine that an organization is running a week-long design workshop with some stakeholders who haven't previously met. If we possessed a satisfaction-o-meter for the whole team, we would see something like this:

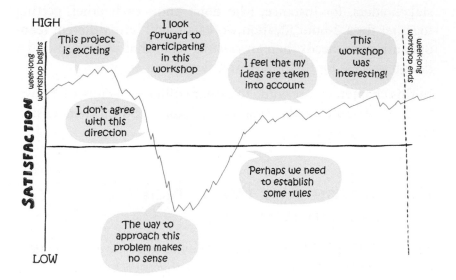

As can be seen, the general mood of the team as well as of each individual varies at different instances. There are moments when team members are excited and fulfilled and others where they feel down and unmotivated. A key reason behind this phenomenon is related to the intricate forces at play during the process of team building.

Psychologist Bruce Tuckman suggested that when teams are developed, they go through different phases. These phases are:

- **Forming**: The team is formed and different team members come together and get to know each other. Uncertainty rises while people look for leadership, coordination, and ways of working together.

- **Storming**: As teams are formed, members start to realize that not all their needs and expectations are being met. Individual members may disagree with team goals, and smaller groups may form around strong personalities or areas of agreement. As a result, potential conflict or friction may lead to frustration, anger, and a drop in performance.

- **Norming**: Teams that manage to deal with conflict, eventually arrive at a point where a group effort is made to resolve problems and achieve group harmony. During this phase, consensus is developed around who takes the lead and individual members' roles, while interpersonal differences start getting resolved.

- **Performing**: In this phase, member collaboration as well as group consensus have been achieved. A set of norms, structures, and relationships has been established, helping teams constructively and efficiently address emerging problems.

All these phases have a special importance and gravity in creating successful and efficient teams. Creative stakeholders come together and discover each other. Conflict may arise due to different perspectives and ways of working, leading to the establishment of new norms, which eventually leads to teams that perform in a new, commonly established, way.

There are several ways to facilitate design team transition among these team development phases during processes and activities. Let's take a look at two of them:

- In the first, special activities can be proposed to facilitate team building and communication during these phases. A classic example of such activities are team-building games, which are designed to help creative stakeholders get to know each other and build relationships between themselves. Another example includes activities around conflict management, trust, or leadership, which are aspects that teams may face during any of their forming, storming, norming, and performing phases. Such activities could potentially address issues related to team performance and dynamics at any given point and help team members deal with conflict or communication issues and to establish a team configuration that helps them achieve their goals.

- In the second way, broader processes address the development and transition between different phases, by adapting their focus based on team maturity. For example, a week-long workshop may present processes where creative stakeholders come together, form, storm, norm, and perform all within

5 days. In order for this to happen, however, the structure of the workshop needs to account for the transition between those phases and have activities that help teams get to know each other at the outset, identify and manage potential conflict, and facilitate their team-building process until they come up with their own norms that will help them perform.

The same principle applies to longer processes, which are built to last for a long period of time, accompanying teams from the beginning to the end of projects. As time passes though, teams transform, they grow, and pass through different phases. As a result, design processes need to take this transformation into account and facilitate the transition by adapting the types of activities and steps they propose, focusing on bringing team members together and helping them work together harmoniously.

8.2 Teams Consist of Creative Stakeholders

Creative stakeholders define the success or failure of teams through their behaviors, attitudes, and actions. It is clear that we all socialize, work, and interact with others in different ways. However, it is possible for every creative stakeholder to be made comfortable through effective design processes. When stakeholders feel secure and comfortable, the possibility that they will express their opinion or be open to others' opinions increases. It is normal that team members who are uncomfortable and unmotivated to participate in their team's activities will be negative, unenergetic, and reluctant to contribute to their teams' shared goals.

Imagine for instance running a workshop with different stakeholders who potentially don't even know each other. There are more or less three scenarios for how this could play out.

- **Case 1**: Participants join a new environment and meet people they're not familiar with. Some of them are reserved and shy. Eventually, the workshop moves on and some participants aren't really active, leading to outcomes that are mediocre at best.

- **Case 2**: The workshop moves on and the discussions arise that create some type of tension or disagreement, rendering participants stressed, anxious, or uncomfortable. This could result in the whole workshop either being interrupted or moving forward with outcomes that may not be agreed upon by all team members.

- **Case 3**: The workshop moves forward, participants get to know each other, they feel comfortable with the overall ambience, and work collaboratively to achieve the goals of the workshop.

Which scenario would you prefer to be in?

The three situations described here show some of the different emotional states of creative stakeholders working in teams. If we were to picture participants' different emotional zones, we could imagine them like this:

In the **comfort zone**, as the name suggests, people feel comfortable. In most cases, people are in their comfort zone when they are familiar with the situation they're facing, they don't feel threatened, and their knowledge, skills, and competences are not challenged. Participants prefer staying in their comfort zone, as this is what feels more natural and secure for them. This also means that if an activity doesn't get them to step outside their comfort zone, some participants may stay passive till the end, as exposing themselves might make them feel uncomfortable. We often see colleagues who don't participate much or at all in team activities and discussions, while others like to speak out at every opportunity they see. The fact that some colleagues aren't that active doesn't necessarily mean that they have nothing to say. Instead, they might be being less active because they prefer to stay in their comfort zone.

Design processes need to encourage and push participants outside their comfort zones. When this happens, people engage in activities that they normally wouldn't, gradually escaping their comfort zones. In this case, the next phase that they may find themselves in is the **stretching zone**. While in the stretching zone, participants have to use their skills and apply their knowledge, they interact with others and, together, they grow. However, if participants are pressed too much, they start feeling uncomfortable, anxious and, eventually, they panic. This emotional state is called the **panic zone**. Design processes should try to not only keep participants active and engaged enough to exit their comfort zone and start performing but also avoid pushing them past their limits, making them panic.

As teams grow and evolve, so do participants and their perceptions about what makes them comfortable and what doesn't. As a result, interaction and participation in design processes eventually moves the boundaries of the comfort, stretching, and panic zones. So, a situation that might potentially stress participants at the beginning of an activity might not after the creative stakeholders have become a team, gotten to know each other, and worked together.

8.2.1 Team Dynamics Is Affected by Team Size and Configuration

When it comes to participation, team size and the type of activity play a big role in how creative stakeholders work and interact. Large team sizes present facilitation complexity while activities and processes with very few participants often come with the danger of not involving all the necessary stakeholders in the decision-making process. So, is there an ideal team size? Well, it all depends on context.

What you need to remember when designing an activity or process is that not all creative stakeholders will participate to the same extent. There are several reasons behind this, including personality, personal reasons, or just the fact that other participants may tend to dominate activities and processes. As a rule of thumb, participation related to group size is like this:

Team Size	Who Participates
3–5 participants	Everyone participates
6–9 participants	Almost everyone participates. Shy participants may participate less and some of them not at all.
10–17 participants	4–5 participants will dominate the activity. Another 4–5 may participate from time to time.
18+ participants	Few people participate

On top of this, there are different personal and interpersonal mechanisms that are activated depending on the nature of each activity. When working individually, we dedicate personal time to finding and solving problems based on our personal ideas, perspective, and experience. When working with others, we present our perspective, receive feedback, and collectively try to find and solve the problems before us.

People who are shy or reserved may feel more comfortable working and thinking individually and in small groups, while others, who are more extrovert, may find it easier speaking and leading the discussion in large groups. This means that, in processes and activities where many people participate, a few people will dominate the discussion while the others may act as observers.

Whether this is a long-term process or a short activity, the number of participants may vary. As a result, activities or processes have to adapt to the dynamics of each situation by breaking up or combining groups of creative stakeholders, providing mechanisms for participants who wouldn't otherwise participate in expressing their perspectives or play a role in the decision-making process.

8.2.2 Good timing and timekeeping plays a big role in team dynamics

Timing is key for smooth processes.

Problem finding and problem solving are complex and mentally demanding processes. Additionally, creative stakeholders need to adapt to the dynamics of the teams they are members of. As we considered before, if we possessed an attention-o-meter during a day-long workshop, it might look something like this:

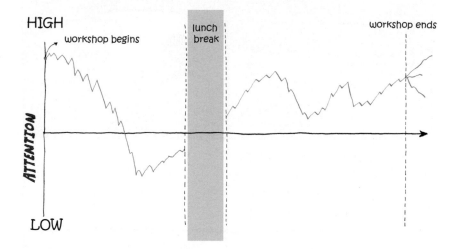

There are moments when participants' attention is set on the objectives at hand, and there are moments when people get tired and easily distracted. After this point, teams may lose focus, get distracted, and discussions may meander, risking participants getting demotivated and doubting the effectiveness of the proposed process. This is why good timing is important: it can optimize processes.

Good timing is linked, but not necessarily limited, to:

- **Good time-keeping**: Have you ever participated in meetings that lasted hours? After such experiences, participants are tired, potentially frustrated, and on the verge of a headache. Good time-keeping is key to getting the most out of creative stakeholders. Meetings that last longer than expected are a great burden on people's attention and energy and may impact the general planning of a broader process. Meetings that are too short for people to discuss and co-create, on the other hand, may not lead to the expected outcomes and may leave participants unsatisfied as they mightn't have contributed the way they wanted to.

- **Understanding the importance of pauses**: Pauses aren't simply important: they are crucial for efficient design processes. They provide creative stakeholders with the opportunity to rest and take a break from intensive and cognitively demanding problem-finding and problem-solving activities. If the activities are facilitated by someone, pauses also provide that facilitator with the necessary time to prepare the next activities.

- **A good balance between intense and fun activities**: Inevitably, team attention and energy will fluctuate during any type of activity. There are moments when teams will be highly concentrated and those when the energy of the team may drop. Participants may start feeling tired or distracted and start speaking to each other about other topics, taking the activity off track. Having more relaxing or fun activities at points like this may prove helpful in getting the team back in the zone. Along with pausing, an activity can be followed up with a short ice-breaking session, during which participants will be detached from the activity they were engaged with. This can increase the energy of participants, bringing them back together, and giving the design process the kick that was needed to move forward.

The Design Process Rectangle

Chapter **9**

How to Read
This Section

DOI: 10.1201/9781003050445-11

Anxious, inexperienced writers obey rules. Rebellious, unschooled writers break rules. Artists master the form.

Robert McKee on storytelling [22]

As there is no single, perfect recipe for successful design processes, this section aims to present insights and best practices on finding the form of your own, individual, and unique design process.

The Design Process Rectangle presents a conceptual, human-centered approach to problem finding and problem solving in design contexts. Its aim is to help design teams to understand the process of problem finding and problem solving through the prism of design and help them come up with their own iterative human-centered design processes.

In Chapter 1 we have established that when formulating a design process nothing is set in stone: your process might (or might not) be based on the structure of the Design Process Rectangle, it may also eventually consist of more or less than four phases, each of which could consist of several substeps. There might come a time where the Design Process Rectangle's Four Fundamental Phases become obsolete for you, as part of the creative stakeholders' continuous self-reflection and search for intrinsically motivating and more efficient work environments.

The chapters that follow aim to present an overview of some tools, methods, and best practices for each phase of the Design Process Rectangle. While **the list is definitely not exhaustive**, they do aim to provide an overview of the aims and structure of each phase.

Don't hesitate to introduce your own tools and methods, to challenge the presented structure and experiment as much as you want in order to arrive at a process that makes sense for you and your teams.

All the elements that we have examined so far culminate in the adjustment of existing design processes or the creation of your own customized ones.

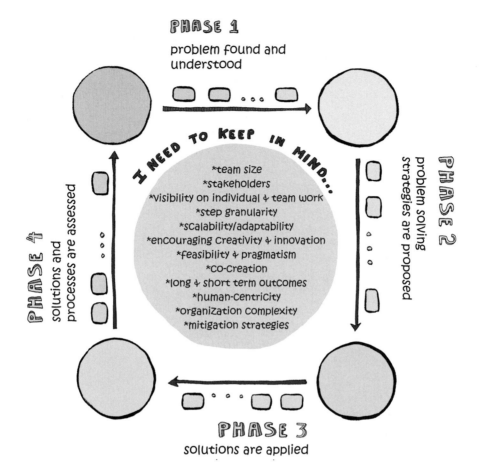

PHASE 1
problem found and
understood

PHASE 2
problem solving
strategies are proposed

PHASE 3
solutions are applied

PHASE 4
solutions and
processes are assessed

I NEED TO KEEP IN MIND...
*team size
*stakeholders
*visibility on individual & team work
*step granularity
*scalability/adaptability
*encouraging creativity & innovation
*feasibility & pragmatism
*co-creation
*long & short term outcomes
*human-centricity
*organization complexity
*mitigation strategies

Chapter 10

Phase 1 - Finding and Understanding Problems

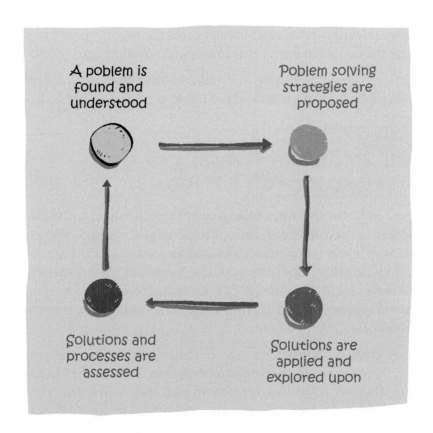

A poblem is found and understood

Poblem solving strategies are proposed

Solutions and processes are assessed

Solutions are applied and explored upon

DOI: 10.1201/9781003050445-12

On a sunny day in May 1934, Tom Carvel was selling ice-cream somewhere around the city of New York, when he got a flat tire. Carvel pulled over and started selling his half-melted ice-cream to bystanders, coming up with the idea of a soft serve ice-cream product. In the midst of his bad luck, Carvel analyzed his environment, identified his available resources under the circumstances, examined his business objectives of selling all his ice-cream stock, and identified the right problem he needed to solve, coming up with a solution.

The first step into design is understanding what problems you need to solve.

However simple or profound this statement may be, it's all too often forgotten. The corporate world and the design industry are full of examples where solutions didn't address users' and organizations' real problems. From the discovery of technologies, which were later unsuccessfully pushed on users who didn't need them in the first place, to lack of business vision, fuzzy UX strategy, and communication problems, focusing on the wrong problem can cause major loss in terms of resources, motivation, and profit.

That's why *Phase 1—Finding and understanding problems* is dedicated to the problems that teams are later asked to solve through design.

10.1 Problem Finding Is an Exploratory Process

We already saw that **one of the greatest enemies of creative stakeholders is their fear of failure**. People who are afraid of making mistakes avoid trying new solutions and ways of working. They tend to do what they already know based on their experiences and the collective knowledge of their teams, even if the results are unsatisfactory. As a result, they forget one of the most important virtues of design: exploration.

When creative stakeholders explore their environment, their products, their resources, the problems they face, and the world around them, they get new ideas, empathize with their users, and identify new problems, which they can later on solve. On top of this, they are open to feedback, ideas, information, and, most importantly, improvement. **Exploration helps us capture the right problems for the right contexts**. Just as it's absurd to expect that Columbus would discover the Americas without ever embarking on an expedition in the first place, it is impossible to expect that the right problems will magically appear in our dreams without us searching for them.

Christopher Colombus

10.2 Facilitating Problem Finding

Explorers need a compass. So do design processes.

No matter how open design processes may be, defining a starting point helps teams have a sense of context and direction. People are more easily aligned when they share the same information and have a clear understanding of the context they are finding problems for or trying to solve. If you have ever participated in teams where you were asked to work on unclear objectives or where different team members had understood the presented problem differently, you are definitely not alone.

As a result, design processes tend to work better when they:

10.2.1 Clearly Communicate Process Goals

I have participated in lots of meetings and workshops where I had absolutely no idea of what they were about and what we needed to accomplish through our participation. Apparently, I was not the only one. This is why the goals of any activity should be clearly explained to creative stakeholders from the beginning of (or even before) each activity. Even if the aims and objectives of an activity or process may be clear to the organizers and facilitators, other team members may have little or no idea about them. For that reason:

- **Don't hesitate to clearly present the goals of the processes and activities you create.**

- **Encourage participants to ask questions and make sure that the goals and instructions of your activities and processes are well understood.**

There are different types of goals. One simple way of categorizing them is:

- **Short-term goals**, which describe the expected outcomes of the team's solutions in the immediate future.

- **Long-term goals**, which describe the expected outcomes of the team's solutions for the future but require time and a set of actions in order to be accomplished.

If, for instance, a team would like to create a new product, some short-term goals might be:

- Understanding the product's audience
- Coming up with some design ideas around the product
- Creating prototypes that could be used to gather initial feedback

Some long-term goals could be:

- Improving user satisfaction
- Increasing user acquisition
- Smoothing platform usability

It's also important to remember that goals are not set in stone. It is possible that throughout the different phases and steps of a design process, goals may change, and problems may be reframed as the result of the exploratory nature of problem finding and problem solving.

There is a huge difference between presenting teams with the goals they need to achieve and explaining how to achieve them. Successful design processes focus on the first aspect: they help creative stakeholders understand why they are participating in an activity or process but don't pose restrictions or push them towards existing solutions, jeopardizing their exploratory and open nature.

REFLECTION POINTS

Are the goals and objectives of your process or activity clear to participants?

- Is the established process itself clear to participants?
- Are participants aware of the resources they have at their disposal during the process?
- Are participants aware of the process breakdown (detailed or generic)? Knowing how a process is structured can help creative stakeholders develop their expectations, understand what is expected of them or how they can contribute, and avoid pointless discussion during various phases around the process structure.
- Have you reserved some time to explain to creative stakeholders the goals of your process?
- Process or activity goals are often set by teams themselves as part of the design process. If this is the case, some time should be dedicated to helping teams come up with their short-term and long-term goals at the beginning of the process.

10.2.2 Present and Capitalize on User Research

Since in the vast majority of cases we are not the users of our products, being able to understand how our users think and interact with our products is of vital importance for our designs. Consequently, design processes should continuously provide creative stakeholders with relevant information, bringing them up to speed and helping them to get a common understanding of the context around which they need to design. Any relevant type of information is helpful at this point, including user research, analytics, business needs, competition overviews, or technical restrictions that absolutely need to be taken into account. Don't hesitate to make a list of the information that creative stakeholders who are participating in a design process need to know.

The best way to understand one's customers and users is by interacting and speaking directly with them. There are several ways to do this, including observing them in their native environment (either home or work), interviewing them, or having them participate in surveys. You are hugely encouraged to leave your office and go out, meet, and interact directly with your users in order to get as much information from them as possible. If your organization has user research teams, this would be a good opportunity to touch base with them and include them in the design process.

In many situations, the information that is provided to creative stakeholders can be immense and overwhelming during workshops or other types of activities and processes. Too much information can work counterintuitively, confusing creative stakeholders or slowing them down. In such cases, process creators will need to select what information should be available at each phase, and in what form, so that creative stakeholders have a good understanding of the context they examine but don't get lost or cognitively overloaded at the same time. For example, there are times where a separate activity dedicated to user research would be necessary in order to prepare creative stakeholders for problem finding and problem solving, while there are others where user research presentation is part of or a substep of other activities, making the appropriate information available at the right time.

REFLECTION POINTS

Are creative stakeholders provided with user research or any other information that will help them make informed decisions?

- Have you identified any source of information that could help you better address the problems you are targeting?

How is the information going to be presented to participants? If there is a lot of information, a coherent and easily digestible way to present it would be necessary.

- Are individual experts going to present information from their field of expertise? In this case, presentations should be time-boxed and focused on relevant information around the addressed problem.
- Is the presentation of user research going to happen as part of an activity or process or will it take place as a preliminary step?
- Is the presentation of user research going to take place in one long session or is it going to be broken down into smaller ones?

Will user research be available to creative stakeholders throughout the whole design process? If yes, are creative stakeholders aware of how to access it when they need it?

10.2.3 Capturing Questions and Finding Problems

Finding and understanding problems requires us to ask questions. The more questions we ask, the better our perspective and understanding on a topic becomes, giving us a better chance to find problems and solve them.

There are several questions that teams can ask at this phase. Some of which may be:

- **Who is your audience?** Being able to identify and empathize with our audience allows us to better understand the needs of our customers and thus propose solutions that better solve their problems.

- **What are your business objectives?** Design is user-centered and business-facilitating. Both of these aspects need to exist in successful and viable products.

- **What are your resources?** What are your team's resources in terms of people, time, budget, tools, content, and technical capabilities?

An interesting way of generating questions is through the **In What Ways Might We** approach. As its name suggests, creative stakeholders start their phrases with "In What Ways Might We" and then add their question. Formulating questions with this approach encourages people to come up with more questions and, later on, potential solutions, which is what this phase is all about.

During this phase, the goal is to aim for quantity and not quality on the questions you pose. As creative stakeholders and their teams propose questions, they start considering different aspects of the problem and its context. The very process of asking questions individually and collectively helps creative stakeholders align on the context they are exploring and build a collective understanding of the problem and the field around it. The team will later have the opportunity to narrow the focus of all the posed questions and elaborate on aspects that they consider worth exploring more.

As questions are posed, creative stakeholders have the opportunity to identify the problems that they need to solve. Consequently, capturing questions is strongly related to problem finding. Eventually, teams need to decide which problems or problem aspects they need to solve. These problems or problem aspects need to be clearly defined, explained, and presented to all team members. This is very important for what comes next, as differing interpretations and understanding of these problems by various team members will definitely create communication issues and friction later on.

REFLECTION POINTS

Try to encourage creative stakeholders to pose as many questions as they can throughout the whole of Phase 1 as well as during the next phases.

Does your process provide creative stakeholders with enough space to pose questions?

Does your process provide creative stakeholders with the opportunity to go through user research, and examine and understand it so that they can pose questions?

Does your process consist of any activity or step during which creative stakeholders can pose questions?

Do creative stakeholders have the time and opportunity to clearly formulate the problems they decide to solve?

Is there a clear and concise presentation of the problems that teams need to solve?

10.2.4 Thirteen Thinking Tools

In their book *Sparks of Genius* [23], Robert and Michelle Root-Bernstein examined the writings of several very creative people aiming to examine and understand their creative thinking processes. As a result, they identified 13 thinking tools that creative people use in their processes, combining their experience, creativity, and intuition.

The 13 thinking tools are very relevant for trying to identify and understand problems. These tools are:

1. **Observing**: Knowledge begins with observation. Observation goes beyond what we see and expands to all our senses. The more we train ourselves to observe, the better we become at it.

2. **Imaging**: We can recall past experiences through mentally visualizing images regarding various fields, such as music, scenery, paintings, and films as well as experiences and interactions with products.

3. **Abstracting**: Creative people critically examine their experiences in order to extract and abstract their core elements, such as ideas, structure, notions, focusing later on their essence.

4. **Recognizing patterns**: When we continuously observe and analyze, we can identify patterns in the topics we examine. We identify patterns in how we work, how technology behaves, and how users perceive and interact with our products.

5. **Forming patterns**: Creative people combine different elements, creating new unforeseen patterns.

6. **Analogizing**: Have you ever found connections and associations between things that were otherwise unrelated? This is analogizing, and it is the creation of analogies that helps us to connect aspects we already know with ones that we want to explore.

7. **Body thinking**: On several occasions, we use our body as a thinking instrument. Dancers may experience and practice a choreography before performing it while pianists may come up with new melodies while tapping on the keys. On some

occasions engaging in physical activities can prove to be very fruitful and should be encouraged in some design activities and processes.

8. **Empathizing**: When we observe the world around us, we start understanding that other people perceive the world around them differently. We familiarize ourselves with their points of view and we become more versed in thinking how they think.

9. **Dimensional thinking**: Sometimes we need to perform mental representations of two- or three-dimensional objects, where we need to alter their proportions, size, and form. This skill is very important for designers.

10. **Modeling**: After we observe and analyze the phenomena that we are interested in, we create models (mental or physical) using some of the tools mentioned above.

11. **Playing**: Play provides a fun and error-free way of approaching rules and procedures, where people are not afraid of failing. Play helps us transform knowledge and acquire a broader understanding of the world around us and the concepts we want to conquer.

12. **Transforming**: Design work requires an ability to find and define problems through some particular tools and explore solutions through others. We may use pattern recognition as a means to identify problems and we may also need to use it to form new patterns.

13. **Synthesizing**: When we bring ideas, memories, and experiences together, we create coherent and holistic perspectives of the experiences we want to design. This is synthesizing.

10.3 Design Processes Use Narratives

One way that we process and understand information is in the form of narratives. We constantly narrate stories to express ourselves and communicate with others. Narratives appear in several aspects of design, from presenting the context that we work in to describing our users, their interactions with our products, and their daily lives.

Narratives, in this way, are a powerful tool for presenting user research, as existing studies can be compiled into a form that is easy for creative stakeholders to follow and remember. When we read or listen to stories, we are also introduced to characters, we empathize with them, we see their problems, and we feel the emotional impact of the events that are presented. As a result, narratives can be used as tools of expression for several aspects of design processes.

Two narrative tools that can be used in this problem-finding phase are:

10.3.1 Personas

One way of describing your audience is through personas. Persona is the Latin word for person or a role, and in the context of design, personas describe fictional characters that represent a typical part of our audience [24]. An interesting and positive aspect of personas is that creative stakeholders tend to focus more easily on characters, whether they are fictional or not, rather than abstract characteristics of their users. By using personas, teams can represent and create a common reference point for several segments of their user base, understanding their individual needs, expectations, and reactions when using products and services.

Personas are effective when:

- **They represent real users, based on user research**. Even if some creative stakeholders may think that they know their audience very well, it is important to point out that we are not our users. Users' habits, needs, and expectations change constantly along with the evolution of technology. No one is more suited to understand and describe users' needs than users themselves. That's why user research is crucial for the creation of personas.

- **The number of personas is limited**. Since all users are unique, design is faced with the challenge of coming up with solutions that address the needs of a broad user base. Personas are proposed as a tool that improves the design process by combining common attributes of users, thus helping design teams address the needs of those groups of users. Having too many personas beats the very purpose of proposing them. As a general rule of thumb, four to five personas are enough for a project. This number, however, heavily depends on the project's scope, needs, and complexity. If, for whatever reason, your audience consists of users who are extremely different from each other and whose characteristics cannot be grouped into a few personas, then it's possible that personas may not be the right tool for your needs.

- **They provide creative stakeholders with as much information as possible regarding the context** that the team is being asked to work in. If, for instance, a design team is working on a learning app focusing on primary school students, the proposed personas could include information such as age, students' access to technology, learning misconceptions, and understanding of the subject matter, learning styles, needs, and expectations.

10.3.2 Journey Maps

Journey maps are visual representations of the processes that different actors go through in order to achieve a goal or a set of goals.

As a result, journey maps are a powerful narrative instrument through which creative stakeholders can tell stories about their audience and the way they live and interact with products, services, and their environment. There are different types of actors whose actions are presented in journey maps, including users (where we call them user journey maps) and customers (called customer journey maps).

The structure and representation of journey maps is very open and depends a lot on the process that needs to be captured, the needs of a project, and the creative stakeholders that are drafting it. Most journey maps, however, contain at least the following components:

- **The actors** = the type or types of users involved in the process described in the journey map.

  We can imagine actors as being the protagonists of the narratives we want to present. There are some who feel that journey maps should focus on only one actor per narrative and others who believe that, depending on the context, having more than one actor (especially if those actors interact with each other) provides a more global perspective of the captured process.

- **The scenario** = the context around which the whole journey map is built.

  The scenario explains the aims, needs, and expectations of a journey map's actors and explains the premise around the visual representation of the journey map.

- **Process breakdown** = the different phases and steps of the process that actors implement to achieve their goals.

  The analysis, breakdown, and structure of a journey map process have several similarities with the process attributes we have previously examined, including length, granularity, and focus.

- **State of mind and emotions** = what actors are thinking and feeling at different instances of the journey.

- **Opportunities** = hints and suggestions that arise throughout the whole journey of mapping process, aiming to help design teams better understand specific problems and situations.

Journey maps can be used in different ways, for example, describing the present mindset, process, and emotions of the involved actors. In cases like this, journey maps are built based on user research and other insights that the team has already gathered and can help as a tool for:

- Capturing questions
- Finding problems
- Creating a common understanding of the examined problem
- Preparing teams by creating a common point of reference for the next phases of the design process

Journey maps can also be used to describe potential solutions to problems. This utility of journey maps has great value, especially during solution exploration and proposal phases, as we will see later on. Journey maps describe potential future solutions in a narrative form by presenting how different customers or users would experience the solutions that design teams want to propose.

Why do we put this process in place in the first place?

What is our process core?

What are the goals of organizing our process or activity? Why are we all participating in it?

Who is participating in this process? Have participants been introduced? Do participants know the role and specialty of the rest of the team?

Is there any information, including user research or analytics that we could use? Is it enough for our process? If not, what actions do we need to take?

How can we bring everyone up to speed regarding user research in a way that doesn't overwhelm or confuse creative stakeholders?

How are we in terms of team dynamics? Is an ice-breaker or an energizer game activity needed?

Who are our users and customers?

What are our audience's needs and expectations?

Can we present in some way what our audience does, thinks and feels?

Can we identify any ways to improve our users' and customers' work or personal experience?

Does our audience face any challenges or issues that we could address somehow? Can we list those challenges?

What questions can we ask regarding the context we examine? Can we list those questions?

Are all participants contributing to the process? How is the dynamics of the team? Is there any action we can take to address communication

What are the problems that we have identified?

How many problems did we identify? If they are a lot, does the team need to make a selection of the problems they want to focus on?

Can we clearly present the problems, issues, processes that the team wants to solve in some way? What way are we going to choose?

Are the identified problems clear to everyone?

Chapter 11

Phase 2 - Coming Up with Problem-Solving Strategies

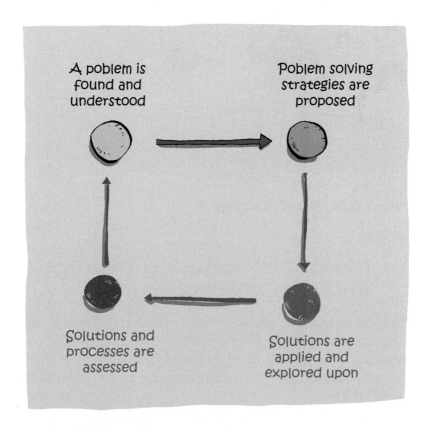

DOI: 10.1201/9781003050445-13

A well-defined starting point and a shared understanding of process goals and context offer creative stakeholders a great kick-start. Teams can now explore different solutions for the problems they have previously defined. When it comes to problem solving, design processes should encourage and facilitate **divergent and convergent thinking.**

Let's examine both of those aspects.

11.1 Divergent Thinking Strategies and Design Processes

Divergent thinking is related to the creative stakeholders' ability to propose multiple and different solutions to given problems. An element of divergent thinking is based on the premise that the more ideas teams have, the more possible it is that some of them may be effective.

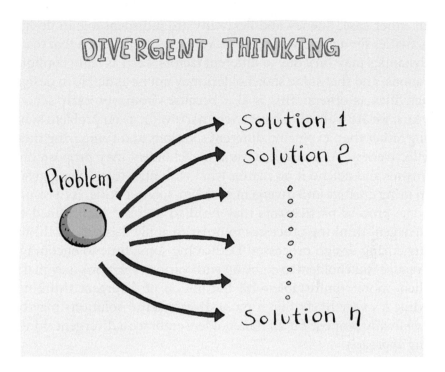

Divergent thinking is strongly related to the following skills of creative stakeholders [25,26]:

- **Fluency**: the ability to produce **many** responses to given situations.

- **Flexibility**: the ability to come up with **different** types of ideas.

- **Originality**: the ability to generate out-of-the-box, **unique,** and not-frequently encountered ideas based on their resources.

- **Elaboration**: the ability to provide a considerable degree of **detail** on their ideas.

There is a great discussion around the connection between fluency and originality. There are researchers who believe that proposing many solutions has a better chance of resulting in original suggestions while there are others who believe a large quantity of answers won't necessarily lead to novel solutions.

In either case, fluency and flexibility are indispensable in design activities for a variety of reasons. We have already seen that team dynamics may vary due to different factors, such as team configurations, and that some stakeholders may not be as active in design activities as others. This is also because, from our early school years, we are trained to have a very narrow focus on problem solving rather than exploring different solutions and comparing their effectiveness. As a result, several stakeholders may propose one answer and defend it no matter what with little focus being given to using creative and divergent problem-solving skills. As a result, some process participants may need to become accustomed to divergent thinking processes in order to apply this type of thinking during design processes. Dedicating some time to encourage creative stakeholders to come up with various solutions may make them more comfortable with the notion of divergent thinking, while it's very likely that a more diverse set of solutions may be eventually proposed if all stakeholders embrace a divergent thinking approach.

Here are some interesting tools related to divergent thinking that you can use:

11.1.1 Brainstorming

Brainstorming is a famous idea generation (idea generation is also called ideation) tool based on Osborn's principle of deferred judgment [27]. The premise behind this principle is that we evaluate ideas **after** a number of them have been generated. According to Osborn, generating ideas and assessing them simultaneously would be like trying to drive while pushing both the gas and the brake pedals.

The premise behind brainstorming is to evaluate ideas after a number of them have been generated!

There are four rules behind brainstorming:

1. **Criticism is not allowed**: Creative stakeholders should not evaluate ideas until all ideas have been proposed. This excludes both verbal and nonverbal communication. When it comes to criticism, there are many ways that it can be communicated, like gestures, facial expressions, or exhaling, which may spoil the very nature of the tool.

2. **Think freely**: Proposals that may seem unfeasible or far-fetched are encouraged in brainstorming, as they hold potential for creative and feasible ideas in the future. Even if these ideas themselves may not be implemented, they may shift the discussion focus towards other directions and inspire other team members, leading to potentially interesting and feasible ideas in the future.

3. **Aim for many proposals**: As we already saw, there is a greater chance of coming up with good ideas when there are more proposals.

4. **Ideas can be combined and improved**: Even if some ideas during brainstorming are themselves interesting, it's good to remember that even better ideas may come from the combination of proposed ideas. Since working collaboratively in teams provides us with the opportunity to view and consult the expertise of our peers, we can get inspired by their proposals and build upon them to propose solutions for the problems we face. This rule, on some occasions, may act as a supplementary step of an initial individual brainstorming round, where creative stakeholders have already thought about different ideas on their own and then try to improve and expand on their ideas by getting inspired by the perspective of others.

There is no single perfect configuration of brainstorming. Team size, context, and topic may require different approaches to brainstorming sessions.

As we already saw, team size plays a big role in team dynamics. Large groups of participants create more complexity when running brainstorming sessions as some participants may dominate the discussion while others may not be as involved. Team dynamics may also be impacted by different team configurations. If, for instance, senior management is present at the discussion, some creative stakeholders may be less eager to participate and express themselves or may tone down their answers in front of the higher-ups. That's why brainstorming sessions can be run with participants working individually but also in groups [28].

Team dynamics and structure need to be taken into account when structuring different brainstorming activities [15]. Considering that **brainstorming activities work best over short time periods** (normally between 5 and 15 minutes), several **smaller brainstorming sessions can be run consecutively** during a design process. For example, creative stakeholders could brainstorm individually for a period of 10 minutes, then present their ideas and then work collaboratively to build upon their collective ideas. There is no limit to the number of iterations of brainstorming activities as long as they don't tire the participants out.

The form of brainstorming activities is also diverse. Creative stakeholders may verbalize, doodle, or write their ideas, using any type of physical or digital instrument that is convenient for each situation. If detail is a quality being sought during a brainstorming activity, fine pens may be a good idea, which contrasts with sessions where more general and abstract concepts are required, where fat markers would be a better choice. Since not all creative stakeholders are comfortable designing, **the design process should make sure that all creative stakeholders feel comfortable** with the process and that they can all express themselves with the tools they have. If there are facilitators of the brainstorming activity, they should present the different options and explain that the aim of these types of sessions is idea generation and not an evaluation of design skills.

Idea presentation is also an important aspect of brainstorming. Creative stakeholders may present their ideas in any way they feel comfortable. On some occasions, they can write their ideas on sheets of paper and present them to their peers, while in other variations they could stick these sheets on the wall and let peers discover the proposed ideas themselves. People can then pass from poster to poster, explore the ideas of their peers, and either build upon them or get inspired for their own work.

Another form of brainstorming focuses on proposing ideas that are the opposite of the desired outcomes. Here, creative stakeholders could propose ways of making a website more complex to use or how to waste resources on a project instead of optimizing them. These are called **reverse brainstorming sessions** and aim to help participants identify and abstract key components of the proposed situation, acquainting themselves with the topic, and potentially discovering new solutions for the desired outcomes of the process as well.

11.1.2 SCAMPER

SCAMPER is a divergent thinking tool, introducing team members to a creative problem-solving process. The tool was proposed by Osborn [29] and was later expanded by Eberle [30].

SCAMPER stands for the following activities:

- **Substitute**: The activity encourages creative stakeholders to come up with equivalent versions of a presented theme. During this activity, creative stakeholders are asked questions like:

  o What materials they could use instead?

  o What other components could their product have?

  o What other services could be proposed?

  We substitute in design every day, since we continuously try to think of alternative solutions for the products we design. We see new releases of apps and websites constantly. During many of these, designers try to propose different variations for the configuration and layout of their designs, which is a form of substitution.

- **Combine**: Combine stands for the process of finding and combining different concepts and ideas in our search for new solutions to our problems. During this phase, creative stakeholders are asked what ideas can be combined with others and what their results would be. We see combination in several aspects of design. Social media platforms may offer gaming, food delivery, dating, or e-commerce services by combining different types of ideas and user needs.

- **Adapt**: When we adapt, we try to change existing and known solutions in order to use them in other contexts we face. Email and instant messaging services came about as an adaption of previous communication models, where people used telephones or postage.

- M can stand for several notions, including **Magnify, Minify, or Modify**. When creative stakeholders **magnify**, they try to see how they could expand and enlarge the characteristics of their products and solutions. They want to explore:

  o How they can scale their business model.

  o How they can get more user traffic.

  o How they can expand the resolution and capabilities of the devices they create.

  When they **minify**, they inversely try to see how they can find more compact solutions to the problems they face, like creating lighter devices or decreasing loading time. **Modify**, on the other hand, is an activity where creative stakeholders try to change the characteristics and attributes of existing ideas, aiming for similar or better results. Such modifications can be about any aspect of a product of service, such as layout, color palette, business model, or technical stack.

- **Put to other uses** is related to creative stakeholders' effort to use existing ideas in new ways. For example, the use of low-tack adhesive glue used to create sticking paper led to the proposal for post-its. Additionally, the expansion of Lego activities to films and video games has led to the proposal of new products and experiences.

- **Eliminate**: Focuses on eliminating and removing elements that are not necessary or have little value for users or organizations. By asking how we can eliminate complexity, reduce the cognitive load of the interfaces we design or remove content that may not be useful, creative stakeholders try to make their designs more efficient through elimination.

- **Rearrange**: Examines the structure and sequence of ideas. When creative stakeholders rearrange, they try to come up with new solutions or ideas by changing the order, frequency, or configuration of components of their products and services.

11.1.3 Creative Pauses

Even if divergent thinking focuses on the proposal of multiple solutions to given problems, it also includes various thinking strategies, one of which is the creative pause. Creative pauses present participants with the opportunity to stop in the middle of their problem-solving process, extend their focus to other perspectives than the ones they are working on, and wonder if there are any alternative points of view for the topics they work on.

There are moments where we focus too much on the topic at hand and we may lose track of the bigger picture.

Creative pauses are useful precisely in cases like this, providing us with the opportunity to review the contexts and problems we are working on and review potential alternative solutions that may be worth examining further.

11.1.4 "What Ifs"

"What Ifs" is a tool based on de Bono's "Use of Po" [31]. The tool provides a generative technique where creative stakeholders propose different ideas by:

- **Exaggerating** existing ideas, where creative stakeholders select one or more characteristics or attributes of the topic they work on and stretch them to unreasonable proportions.

In this way, potential attributes and aspects of the examined theme may come out or the magnifying or diminishing of the aspects covered by creative stakeholders may highlight processes that could be used to solve the problems that teams face.

- **Inverting** situations, during which creative stakeholders select elements and attributes of situations they face and turn them inside-out. If for instance, a startup, let's call it "StartUp," was to launch a new product, called Product X, that would be directly or indirectly competing with an existing product, the competitors could, in their divergent thinking process, pose the question: "What if Product X was launched by us instead of StartUp?" In that way, the competitors could start thinking about the impact and potential reactions that an inverse situation would have on Product X, helping them come up with some potentially helpful ideas that they could explore further.

- **Distorting** situations, during which creative stakeholders alter elements, interactions, or relationships in order to explore different possibilities. For organizations, where few stakeholders put any emphasis on design for instance, a distorting "What If" could be: "What if all stakeholders, including upper management, participated in ideation sessions?" In this way, current concepts and ways of working are challenged in order to create a potentially better work environment.

11.1.5 Removing Mental Barriers in Design Processes

As problem solving has consistently been studied through various scientific fields, psychologists have identified several thinking aspects that impede efficient problem solving. Two of those aspects, pointed out by Gestalt psychology, are **entrenchment** and **functional fixedness**.

Sometimes prior knowledge may impact the way we solve problems in a negative way. As we learn and grow up, we construct our own personal mental models, which are our own mechanism for processing knowledge and understanding the world around us.

As a result, we also develop experiences and approaches to several aspects of our personal and professional lives, which mean we often apply a known or "standard" (for us) solution to a problem, while there could be a simpler and more efficient one if we really focused on how we already get things done. This is called **entrenchment**.

Applying knowledge and process that we already know to problems we face is highly useful in the majority of cases. It would be unwise to try reinventing the wheel for every problem we ever face. On some occasions however, habit or existing mental models can set a team's focus on a solution which could be inefficient or even wrong. As a result, design processes need to provide creative stakeholders with the opportunity to take "fresh" looks at the problems they face, detaching themselves from entrenchment.

Functional fixedness is another form of mental barrier where we are unable to figure out how we could use components or objects in our problem-solving process in ways other than their initial design purpose. As we already saw before during George Land's paper clip experiment, students were asked to list as many potential uses of a paper clip as they could, a skill that decreased as the students grew up. Functional fixedness makes us focus on the main functionality of a tool, product, or element which leads us to neglect other potential uses that may help us solve problems that we face.

If we consider that during design creative stakeholders are continuously asked to come up with elaborate and innovative solutions, often in situations with limited resources, functional
fixedness may have a negative impact on a design team's output.
Approaches where creative stakeholders need to improvise, adapt

to dire circumstances, or use minimal resources, such as the French Système D or Indian Jugaad are based on reducing functional fixedness as much as possible.

11.2 Convergent Thinking and Design Processes

Convergent thinking is related to taking concrete and deliberate decisions. When we apply convergent thinking, we examine ideas through various criteria, we analyze them and assess them, trying to come up with the best potential solutions for the problems we are asked to solve.

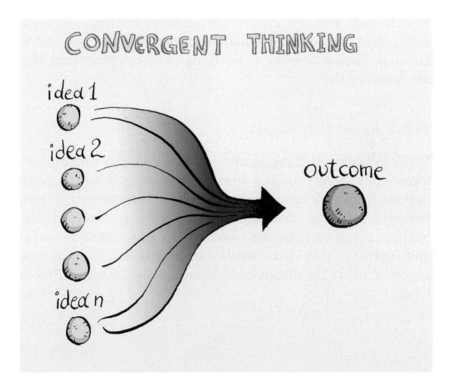

So, while in divergent thinking we strive for diversity, quantity, innovation, and thinking outside the box, in convergent thinking we try to dissect and analyze the problems that we are presented with and narrow down different ideas, coming up with the best possible responses for the situations we are presented with. Narrowing down and choosing between different solutions isn't always easy; decision-making requires us to filter both our ideas and the ideas of our peers in a logical and impartial manner. That would make sense if we all shared the same perspective, criteria, and understanding of the context we are dealing with. However, stakeholders with different types of expertise join design processes with different mental models. For instance, developers, designers, and product managers have different priorities and understandings of what is feasible or not from the perspective of their field. As a result, from their own point of view, each of them may be right.

You can imagine that such types of situations may drive teams to dead ends and cost creative stakeholders endless discussions with potentially no shared outcomes or decisions. So, how can we facilitate efficient convergent thinking in design processes? Here are some key tips:

11.2.1 Assessing Ideas

While in divergent thinking, the goal is to come up with multiple ideas, convergent thinking aims at narrowing down proposed options, helping design teams to choose between the best of them. However, assessing ideas depends on several factors, including business objectives, user and customer needs, available resources, and context-related characteristics or limitations. Most of these aspects should have already been defined through a team's Process Core.

Depending on team structure and dynamics giving and receiving feedback on different ideas may vary. There are creative stakeholders who prefer being direct and confrontational and others who don't and would prefer holding back on their ideas to keep things smooth during exchanges of feedback. For this reason, such activities could span from simple presentations of creative stakeholders' ideas and then discussing, critiquing, and assessing different ideas to putting post-its about different ideas up on the wall. In any case though:

- **Feedback needs to be constructive**. Being able to identify flows can be very helpful but also catastrophic in design contexts. Provided feedback needs to point out issues along with suggestions about how to address those issues, creating a proactive discussion and not a competition about which creative stakeholder will find the most flaws in their peers' proposals.

- **Such activities need to be well facilitated and time-framed** in order to avoid endless discussions, potential meandering, and not delivering value for the team and process goals.

- **The focus isn't validating or invalidating ideas but identifying which ideas or components of these ideas could better address a team's given problem**. If an overall idea isn't deemed interesting by a team but a specific aspect is, this aspect can be taken apart and worked upon or combined with other ideas.

Since convergent thinking is about selecting the best solutions based on one's analysis and criteria, there is no better tool to help creative stakeholders in this endeavor than user research. User research encompasses all different types of studies and ways to get information about our users, their habits, preferences, attitudes, interaction with our products, as well as usability issues. User research can also take different forms, presenting us with quantitative information, like how many users enter and exit one's website or how much they convert, as well as qualitative information, like why users exit one's e-commerce website at a specific page or how they perceive the information presented at a specific screen of a mobile application.

Analyzing and reviewing user research can help us come up with insights on how to approach the ideas that we have previously come up with. If, for instance, solutions applied had a positive or negative impact on the designed products or services, user research could help creative stakeholders filter the effective or ineffective ideas. Another example of how user research could help design teams make informed decisions are user interviews and analytics, presenting trends, preferences, and attitudes, which could be used to filter some of the ideas that have been previously proposed.

Teams may have endless discussions about the various opinions and ideas presented during different activities. Developers may focus on feasibility issues related to the selection of an organization's technical stack, project managers may point out that projects are running out of budget, and designers may emphasize the product's aesthetic appeal and usability aspects. Even among members of the same specialty, such as designers, there often may be disagreement on the vision and direction of the projects they are working on. Such situations can lead to endless discussions, where the subjective opinion of one creative stakeholder goes up against that of another.

Even if different creative stakeholders may think they're right in their own heads, one thing is certain: **no one knows which idea works best unless they test them with real users**. Testing is beneficial for design processes in several ways. First of all, it reminds creative stakeholders who their users are and how they really interact with their products, refocusing the discussion around their audience. All too often, decisions are taken by experts who believe that they know how their users think and work. It turns out that on many many (yes, two manys) occasions, this is not the case. As a result, creative stakeholders take design decisions based on their fuzzy perception of their users, leading to solutions that are not efficient or not at all usable. Testing helps creative stakeholders reframe and reconnect with their users.

An outcome of testing with real users is the reduction of long discussions, since creative stakeholders can see at first hand the outcomes of each idea they test. Subjective opinions and points of view are now examined in practice, rendering potential discussions and disagreements around them moot.

At every opportunity, testing is always a good idea.

11.2.2 About Consensus and Voting

Without doubt, when multiple creative minds work together, many solutions and ideas may be proposed. There are several ways to reach decisions when there is more than one possible solution on the table. These include:

- One or more stakeholders making the decision. These stakeholders may be someone's clients, executives, or managers.

- Voting, where creative stakeholders vote for the ideas that they prefer to explore further.

- Arriving at a shared consensus on the solution or solutions to be examined further by the team.

Selecting the best way to reach decisions depends a lot on the project, context, and team configuration. For instance, when the decision-making process depends on one or more executive stakeholders, such as a manager or a CEO, or on a voting session among team members, reaching decisions is usually faster compared to consensus building. On the other hand, it is possible that in the first two cases a segment of the team may not be aligned with the selected solutions, leading to potential further discussions and friction after the completion of a design process or activity, which would be largely avoided through consensus building though it may take longer to achieve.

What is important though is that during convergent thinking sessions teams also start shaping a common understanding of problems and of the solutions that would best address them. This consensus building process helps creative stakeholders to transition from a personal and individual perspective of a good solution to a collective understanding and consensus around the actions decided upon during design activities. **Testing is a key aspect for achieving consensus**, since it helps team members examine the impact of their proposals and see with their own eyes which elements work and which don't.

11.2.3 Co-creation Doesn't Always Mean Co-decision

Even if design is a team sport, decisions aren't always taken by everyone. Due to organizational structure, team configuration, or working with external clients, it is possible that the final decisions may be taken by only a few creative stakeholders of the design process. Does this mean that all collaborative work done so far goes to waste? Absolutely not.

As we just looked at, effective design processes should focus on establishing common understanding and direction on the proposed design process and next steps. Through divergent thinking, all creative stakeholders have the opportunity to express themselves and present various and diverse ideas, which are potentially going to influence and inspire the decision makers participating in the process. This is also the reason why design processes should make sure that all creative stakeholders have the opportunity to present their ideas before the converging processes start. In that way, people can express their ideas, vision, and potential skepticism without being influenced negatively or positively by the opinion and preferences of decision makers.

Last but not least, design processes provide creative stakeholders with learning and transforming experiences. Even if we don't realize it, by participating in design activities, we get influenced by others, and eventually, we slowly change our perspectives regarding the problems we face. This transformation may not necessarily be visible during one iteration, but it may impact future ones or be applied in other situations.

The structure and configuration of the decision-making process should be made clear to participants from the outset, explaining the importance of diversity in creative problem-solving processes as well as managing the expectations of creative stakeholders joining the process.

11.2.4 Converging Doesn't Necessarily Kill Diverging

We already saw that by aiming for quantity during divergent thinking sessions, we potentially increase the possibilities of coming up with some interesting solutions to our problems. During design processes, some stakeholders feel that while converging, as some of their ideas are not eventually considered, the whole divergent thinking part has been a waste of time.

This sentiment absolutely makes sense if the connection between divergent and convergent thinking isn't clear to participants in the process. Divergent and convergent thinking are two aspects of a broader problem-solving process. Even if creative stakeholders are asked to narrow down the ideas they have come up with during convergent thinking sessions, the ideas they have produced aren't dead. The very process of divergent thinking introduces people to the problem, the context around it, and encourages them to start thinking about potential solutions. Creative stakeholders start thinking of ideas, which potentially merge and become a common ground for the whole team. Even if some of the original ideas aren't used later on, they have potentially merged into others, inspired and changed people's minds, and may potentially be used in future sessions or directly or indirectly applied to other products.

Keeping track of the different ideas that come up during divergent and convergent thinking sessions is a good technique for helping creative stakeholders to remember and potentially refer to these ideas in the future.

REFLECTION POINTS

Does your process encourage divergent thinking?

- Is the notion of divergent thinking clear to creative stakeholders? If not, are there any activities or briefings around the goals and value of using this approach in the design process?
- Do any of the proposed activities encourage participants to come up with multiple solutions to given problems?
- Do any of the proposed activities encourage participants to come up with different kinds of solutions?
- Do any of the proposed activities push participants to think of one-of-a-kind ideas?
- Do participants have the time and opportunity to explain their ideas in detail, when needed?

- How many and what types of activities have been selected in the scope of divergent thinking?
- Will the team apply an analytical, synthetical way of approaching the given problems, or both?
- How long will these activities be?
- What are the team dynamics during these activities? Are there any actions that can be taken to address friction, lack of participation, or communication issues?

Does your process encourage convergent thinking?

- Are there any activities proposed in order to assess proposed ideas?
- Are the elements of the Process Core known to all the participants?
- What are participants' criteria for assessing the proposed ideas?
- Is constructive feedback encouraged?
- Are feedback activities time-framed?
- How is the team going to decide which ideas are going to be further explored?
- Are all proposed ideas and the delivered feedback logged? It's possible that some of these ideas may be used in a future iteration.

Chapter 12

Phase 3 – Applying and Exploring Solutions

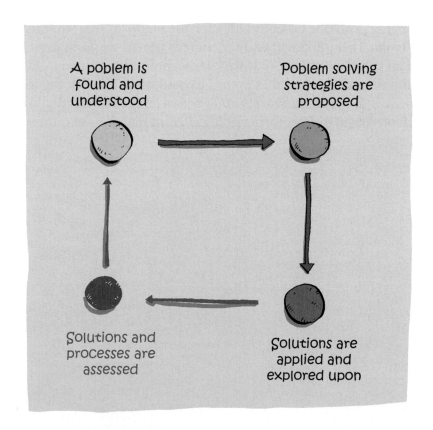

DOI: 10.1201/9781003050445-14

As the French say, when making crepes, the first ones always get burnt! Apart from a great cooking tip, this phrase contains a very important truth: **in the same way that you don't know if a recipe on a page leads to a tasty outcome, you never know how ideas will really work out unless you implement them.**

12.1 The First Step in Solution Application and Implementation Is Communication

A few years ago, I was running a design activity, where several stakeholders, including designers, developers, project managers, and subject matter experts, were invited. By the end of the activity, we had finished brainstorming and eventually decided to focus our efforts on one collective idea for the platform that we wanted to build. Then, different team members started working together on an initial prototype that we later wanted to test. It was at this point that we realized that even if we had come up with the solution together, several aspects and parameters of the solution were still perceived differently between different members of our team.

Design is a team activity that requires the collaboration and mutual understanding of different types of experts who, on many occasions, don't necessarily share the same perspective and understanding of each other's fields. At this phase, it is still possible that even after all the discussions and exchanges during previous phases, stakeholders may not necessarily have the exact same vision for the selected solution.

That's why solutions need to be shared and clearly understood by all team members of a design process.

This means that all team members need to have a common understanding of the solutions they previously agreed to explore. As a result, clear communication and description of the proposed solutions needs to be established before moving forward with implementation. There are several ways that this can happen. I find narratives a very powerful tool in that regard.

We already explored narratives during Phase 1, where we talked about personas and journey maps. Through different types of narratives, creative stakeholders can co-conceive stories that present the solutions they want to address. In that way, the team has the opportunity to discuss, clarify issues regarding the solution they want to propose, and establish a common understanding of their proposal. Narratives can also be used to explain this solution to other stakeholders who may be directly or indirectly involved in implementing this solution.

Shared and clear understanding between creative stakeholders doesn't necessarily mean that each and every aspect of the proposed solution is clearly defined.

The field of design is often connected with ambiguity, due to the complex and continuously evolving nature of the context that we face. Especially during early design and development phases, it is very likely that some solution parameters may be ambiguous or even not yet defined. This very fact may be beneficial where teams may want to explore solutions for system components or focus only on specific cases, confirming or rejecting their hypothesis without going deeper into every concept they want to explore. It allows teams to explore different solutions, failing or succeeding fast and early and learning from each iteration and effort they make in order to continuously improve their solution strategies.

As a result, design processes focus on helping team members acquire the same understanding of the solutions they want to explore by making it clear which aspects of the solution are going to be implemented and which aspects remain ambiguous or not defined at each stage.

REFLECTION POINTS

Does your process establish a common understanding of the solution between different stakeholders?

- Are the proposed solutions that came up during Phase 2 clearly defined?
- Are those solutions presented in a way that is clear and accessible to all creative stakeholders?
- Would a journey map or any other tool help illustrate and explain the proposed solutions?
- Are there aspects that haven't been defined yet in the examined solutions? Ambiguity is a natural aspect of design. However, all process participants need to have an understanding of which aspects are defined and which are not.

12.2 Exploring Different Solutions

The sooner we test our ideas, the easier it is to see if they work.

Sometimes organizations and teams wait till their solutions become mature and already well developed before presenting them to users, if at all. The biggest issue behind this practice is that these ideas may not have been worth exploring further in the first place. As a result, resources, effort, and motivation, which would be otherwise invested in more fruitful directions, are dedicated to activities without the expected outcomes.

This is the reason why we should test with real users as early as possible with the resources we have so we can get feedback about our ideas as soon as possible. The following are some tips about exploring and applying different solutions:

12.2.1 Test, Test, Test!

> There are not enough words to express the importance of testing in design processes.

Design processes need to encourage testing from the earliest to the latest phases of product development, from concept to release. Creative stakeholders can test their ideas and hypotheses in many ways, including technical feasibility, business value proposition, usability, conversion, or retention. Testing with real users and customers is and should be a team's first priority when it comes to testing.

12.2.2 What Type of Prototypes Are You Aiming For?

There are different ways of testing our design solutions, and they don't all require tremendous design skills or elaborate graphics. For starters, we could categorize prototypes into the following two categories:

1. **Low-fidelity prototypes**, which can be either paper or digital based. Low-fidelity prototypes aim to present the proposed solutions without necessarily dedicating the effort that would be necessary for a more elaborate implementation. These prototypes use basic shapes and content in order to convey the essence of the proposed solutions. In most cases, coming up with low-fidelity prototypes is faster than producing high-fidelity ones, giving teams the opportunity to test faster, get feedback, perform adjustments and re-test.

2. **High-fidelity prototypes** are in most cases digital based. High-fidelity prototypes aim to provide an accurate representation of the proposed solutions. As a result, they present

graphics and interactive functionalities that are closer to the envisioned end result. For that reason, more time and design and development work are required for their production. Since high-fidelity prototypes try to emulate the envisioned solutions, the feedback received during testing them can provide invaluable insights into how to improve the ideas that teams are working on.

12.2.3 Approximation Is Stronger Than Perfection

Have no fear of perfection; you will never reach it.

Salvador Dali

There is no single recipe for perfection, since perfect answers don't exist. We already saw that we are all different: we perceive our world in different ways, we have different priorities and different needs, making us unique. Even if we could design solutions that address the unique needs of each one of our customers and users, it still wouldn't be enough, since these people evolve and grow every day. Being part of various cultures and societies, we continuously interact with other people, technologies, and our environment. Hence, our needs today may be different from those of tomorrow, rendering products, tools, and previous ways of working redundant.

Through design processes, creative stakeholders try to address organization and user needs through solutions that they envision through problem finding and problem solving. The iterative nature of such processes presents teams with the opportunity to get closer to addressing those needs by improving or building upon the solutions that teams explore through continuous design approximations.

Continuous design approximations describe our effort to come closer to envisioned solutions that address and fulfill an organization or user's needs one iteration at a time. Since we have established that perfect solutions don't exist and that user and organization needs are prone to change continuously, through continuous approximations we try to arrive at solutions that increasingly close in on the problems and situations that design teams need to solve.

Are the proposed solutions clear to all creative stakeholders?

Which aspects of each solution are defined and which aren't?

Are there any communication issues during idea exploration and application? If yes, are there any envisioned corrective actions?

What are the criteria based on which the team is going to assess their ideas?

What type of prototypes is the team aiming for?

Chapter 13

Phase 4 - Assessing Solutions and Processes

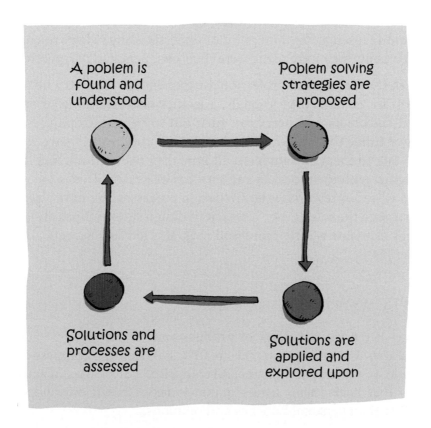

A poblem is found and understood

Poblem solving strategies are proposed

Solutions and processes are assessed

Solutions are applied and explored upon

DOI: 10.1201/9781003050445-15

Even if it's sometimes neglected as a step, **assessment is invaluable for the viability of any creative problem-solving process.** The main argument behind evaluation is that design teams don't really know if they have successfully solved the problems they embark on solving without examining the impact and efficiency of their problem-solving process.

In this chapter, we are going to explore how to assess both solutions and processes and see how design teams can improve their overall efficiency through establishing efficient and effective evaluation approaches.

13.1 Solution Assessment

Have you ever participated in an activity or process where creative stakeholders couldn't agree with each other? Even more, have you ever been trapped in endless discussions where stakeholders couldn't reach a common point of understanding, where the only arguments they were using were their own personal perspectives?

Even if personal and professional experience can be very helpful tools for creative professionals, a lack of understanding of one's real customers and users can turn out to be catastrophic. Even if we think that we know our users, we aren't really sure until we talk to them and understand how they really think, feel, and interact with the products and services we design. This is the reason why user research is key in design processes. We have already discussed the role of user research in design several times already. Let's elaborate a little more and look at a few key aspects about user research:

13.1.1 What Is User Research?

One of the main aspects of product and service design is user research. User research is the creative stakeholder's compass in a world of infinite possibilities and comprises a diverse set of activities that help design teams make decisions based on evidence rather than personal hunches and opinions.

There are several ways of conducting user research, including:

Qualitative research, which tries to answer questions like "Why?" (e.g. Why do users leave a purchase funnel at a specific step?) and "How?" (e.g. How do travel agents make a reservation on the platforms they use?). There are several methods of conducting qualitative research, including:

- **Usability testing**, which describes a set of activities during which participants are presented with one or more designs and are asked to perform a set of tasks, while creative stakeholders observe their actions. Usability testing can be both qualitative and quantitative, and we will examine it as a method in a specially dedicated section later on.

- **Interviews**, which describe different types of activities where creative stakeholders ask users one or more questions about the topics they want to know more about. This includes their interests, brand perception, expectations, needs, and issues they face.

- **Field research**, which describes a set of activities that are conducted at a user's work or home environment. In contrast to running studies in a lab or at a design team's office, field research provides invaluable insights on how users work and perform in a real context.

- **Focus groups**, during which participants (usually the number of participants spans from five to nine) gather together and give feedback on existing products or future designs.

Quantitative research, which tries to answer to questions like "How much?" or "How many?" (e.g. How many users make a purchase after entering a website? How much time do users need to make a purchase?). Quantitative research includes methods like:

- **Surveys:** aimed at gathering information about one's users.

- **Analytics:** which provides information about users' interaction with products and services.

- **A/B or multivariate testing:** which aims to provide insights into how users interact with two or more versions of given designs.

Qualitative and quantitative user research offer different perspectives to the process of design, and, as a result, both of them are invaluable. Depending on the questions that design teams may have at different phases of the design process, it's possible that different user research tools may be needed, applying both qualitative and quantitative research methodologies. **If your team and organization has user researchers, their participation in all design activities would be strongly encouraged** in order to help them understand and propose the best user research tools and approaches for each individual situation.

Qualitative research answers to questions like:

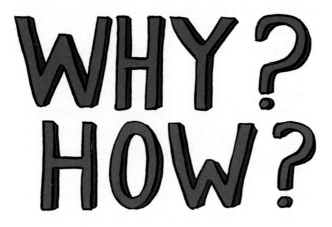

Quantitative research answers to questions like:

13.1.2 What Is Usability Testing?

Usability testing is probably one of the cornerstones of product and service design, due to the method's ability to present creative stakeholders with how users think and interact with their products.

During usability testing sessions, a usability expert (also called a user researcher) presents users with one or more designs and asks them to perform a set of tasks. The researcher observes and takes notes on what users say and do, trying to understand how they think, how they perceive the presented interfaces, and which aspects are unclear or confusing.

Usability testing can take many forms. Usability testing sessions can for instance be:

- Moderated or unmoderated
  - **Moderated**, during which a researcher facilitates the session, taking notes, intervening when users are stuck or confused, and asking questions when considered necessary.
  - **Unmoderated** aren't facilitated by a researcher and during them users receive instructions about the tasks they need to complete through software solutions. As a result, users complete such types of usability testing sessions on their own. Their actions are recorded, allowing researchers to analyze them later on.

MODERATED USABILITY TESTING SESSION

UNMODERATED USABILITY TESTING SESSION

- Remote or on-site

  ○ **Remote**: during which the researcher and the user connect to the session from two different locations. In cases like this, the usability test is conducted though a video-conferencing tool

  ○ **On-site:** during which the researcher and the user are physically located at the same place.

Usability tests should be conducted **with real users**. This is because any other approximation of a design team's audience may be biased or based on false assumptions about their user base. I occasionally meet stakeholders who propose internal usability testing, where participants are going to be other team designers or developers. Apart from a case where the final product's users will be these very designers and developers, **internal usability testing is a bad idea.** Usually creative stakeholders possess a more advanced skillset, as well as an understanding of a product and how it works compared to the average user. As a result, by running usability tests with experts rather than real users, it's highly likely that the design direction will be geared towards power users, rendering the final solution unusable for the broader product or service audience.

There's no time when usability tests aren't relevant! Teams can conduct usability tests from the very early stages of product design up to and after their release. Usability tests can be used to confirm or reject an initial concept hypothesis, examine the validity of low- and high-fidelity prototypes, or assess the usability of finalized products.

13.1.3 Omitting the Step of User Research Leads to Many Backwards Steps

A very common counterargument to conducting user research is that it takes time, slowing down product and service delivery. While this argument may have some grounds in the short term, it is counterproductive in the long term.

The idea of solution assessment in general as part of iterative problem-solving processes is that teams fail fast and fail often, giving them the opportunity to explore various solutions and get feedback as soon as possible, avoiding investing time, resources, and effort into directions that may have no value for users and the organization.

The fact that people are physically located in the same room, reading or listening to the same information doesn't mean that they have the same understanding of an activity and the problem it aims to solve.

Consequently, omitting user research renders the design team blind as there is no information about how their designs impact on users. As a result, the probability of working on inefficient design solutions increases, while the effort and cost of correcting that course of action increases as well. Logically, it's much easier to correct designs drafted on paper rather than designs that have already been coded.

13.1.4 The Bus Accident Paradigm

Imagine that the entire user or customer research team of an organization was taking a walk on a sunny day when... Blam... they get hit by a bus. In the unfortunate event that the whole team is knocked out of action for a long period of time, what would happen to the user research that was conducted in the past? Would the rest of the design team know where to find it? Is it even accessible to them? Would it be clear enough to creative stakeholders so that they could make informed decisions based on it?

The bus accident paradigm aims to highlight that user research should always be available and accessible to everyone inside the organization, maintaining a proper information flow and helping establish collective knowledge between stakeholders.

13.2 Process Assessment

Since design teams are part of an ever-changing world, design processes need to be able to evolve and adapt to the needs of creative stakeholders, businesses, and users.

Aspects that may be felt to have been dealt with during a previous iteration, may change during a later one just because the context or business and user needs have evolved. As a result, there may never be a perfect process as context, audience, resources, and teams constantly evolve.

Design processes however can also continuously evolve in order to help teams solve the problems before them. For processes to become more effective and efficient after each iteration, they need to be examined, assessed, and improved based on the issues that have been identified.

Process assessment can focus on several aspects, including:

- **Team happiness**: How happy are the creative stakeholders participating in the design process? We have already established that the most important aspect of design processes are creative stakeholders. Design processes need to maintain balance between the creative stakeholders' work and personal goals as well as facilitating team development and dynamics, addressing potential friction and miscommunication issues.

- **Team communication**: Working in teams isn't always easy. Bringing together people from different backgrounds and specialties, whose perspective of the same topic varies, it is possible that friction and conflict may arise. The aim of this aspect is to identify issues related to communication and to help design teams address them as soon as possible.

- **Team effectiveness**: This aspect explores whether or not teams manage to achieve the tasks they were supposed to.

- **Team efficiency**: While teams may be able to solve problems, this doesn't necessarily mean that they do it in the most optimum way possible. Team efficiency aims to discover if the team could improve and optimize their design process.

REFLECTION POINTS

Not conducting user research is like flying an airplane with no instruments. The benefits of running it outweigh its potential time and costs, especially if research is conducted efficiently.

- What are your team's questions? Do you write them down and share them somewhere?
- What types of user research studies could address your team's questions?
- Does your team have a user researcher?
- Are there any external user research, consumer insights, customer experience, or analytics teams in your organization? If yes, does your team collaborate with them? If not, how could your team's collaboration with them increase?
- Does your process provide creative stakeholders with the opportunity to reflect upon their workflow, the process itself, and the way they collaborate? Is this reflection taken into account later on to improve the design process or any other aspects raised by stakeholders?

The Creative Stakeholder's Journey

Chapter **14**

The Final
Chapter

DOI: 10.1201/9781003050445-17

Design processes are very much connected with an organization's ability to adapt and deal with change.

While change isn't always easy, it does entail some sort of adventure, which each and every creative stakeholder directly or indirectly embarks on. Every design situation, context, team, and organization is unique and requires different approaches, solutions, and application methods.

Even if tweaking and adapting existing and industry-established processes may sometimes be the way to go, there are occasions where a more drastic approach may be necessary, where a new, bespoke process is set up from scratch.

In any case, completing one's journey requires self-awareness. As a result, setting up design processes are great opportunities for teams and organizations to self-reflect upon their structure, interactions, and function. By the end, design teams that embark on the journey of establishing their own process will be very different from where they were the day they started off. Even if there may never be an ideal design process, reflecting upon and challenging one's process is a powerful way of moving forward.

Even if this is the end of the ride for this book, a new journey begins, full of new challenges, adventures, and opportunities!

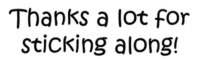

References

[1] J. T. Dillon, 'Problem finding and solving', *The Journal of Creative Behavior*, vol. 16, no. 2, pp. 97–111, 1982, doi: 10.1002/j.2162–6057.1982. tb00326.x.

[2] J. W. Getzels, 'Creative thinking, problem-solving, and instruction', *Theories of Learning and Instruction*, vol. 63, pp. 3–30, 1964.

[3] J. E. Pretz, A. J. Naples, and R. J. Sternberg, 'Recognizing, defining, and representing problems', *The Psychology of Problem Solving*, vol. 30, no. 3, pp. 3–30, 2003.

[4] M. D. Mumford and M. S. Connelly, 'Leaders as creators: Leader performance and problem solving in ill-defined domains', *The Leadership Quarterly*, vol. 2, no. 4, pp. 289–315, 1991.

[5] J. Dewey, *How We Think: A Restatement of the Relation of Reflective Thinking to the Educative Process*. Boston, MA: Houghton Mifflin, 1933.

[6] G. Wallas, *The Art of Thought*. New York: Harcourt, Brace and Company, 1926.

[7] E. P. Torrance, 'The nature of creativity as manifest in its testing', in *The Nature of Creativity: Contemporary Psychological Perspectives*, New York: Cambridge University Press, 1988, pp. 43–75.

[8] G. Polya, *How to Solve It: A New Aspect of Mathematical Method*, Princeton, NJ: Princeton University Press, 1945.

[9] S. J. Parnes, *The Magic of Your Mind*, Buffalo, NY: Creative Education Foundation, 1981.

[10] Design Council, 'What is the framework for innovation? Design Council's evolved Double Diamond', Nov. 11, 2020. https://www.designcouncil.org.uk/news-opinion/what-framework-innovation-design-councils-evolved-double-diamond.

[11] E. Ries, *The Lean Startup*, New York: Crown Publishing Group, 2011.

[12] V. Google, 'The Design Sprint', https://www.gv.com/sprint/ (accessed Nov. 08, 2020).

[13] H. A. Simon, *The Sciences of the Artificial*, Cambridge, MA: M.I.T. Press, 1969.

[14] T. Both and D. Baggereor, 'Design Thinking Bootcamp Bootleg', https://dschool.stanford.edu/resources/the-bootcamp-bootleg (accessed Oct. 29, 2020).

[15] A. J. Starko, *Creativity in the Classroom: Schools of Curious Delight*, 4th ed., New York, London: Routledge, 2010.

[16] G. T. Doran and others, 'There's a SMART way to write management's goals and objectives', *Management Review*, vol. 70, no. 11, pp. 35–36, 1981.

[17] G. Land and B. Jarman, *Breakpoint and Beyond: Mastering the Future Today*, New York: Harper Business, 1993.

[18] J. Piaget, *Play, Dreams and Imitation in Childhood*, New York: W W Norton & Co., 1952.

[19] J. Schell, *The Art of Game Design: A Book of Lenses*, Amsterdam: CRC Press, 2014.

[20] G. Kalmpourtzis, *Educational Game Design Fundamentals: A Journey to Creating Intrinsically Motivating Learning Experiences*, New York: A K Peters/CRC Press, 2018.

[21] M. Csikszentmihalyi and R. Larson, *Flow and the Foundations of Positive Psychology*, vol. 10. Netherlands: Springer, 2014.

[22] R. McKee, *Story: Substance, Structure, Style and the Principles of Screen Writing*, New York: Regan Books, 1997, doi: 10.1016/S0006-291X(05)80899-X.

[23] M. Root-Bernstein and R. Root-Bernstein, *Sparks of Genius: The Thirteen Thinking Tools of the World's Most Creative People*, Boston, MA: Houghton Mifflin Harcourt, 2013.

[24] A. Cooper, *The Inmates Are Running the Asylum*, Indianapolis, IN: SAMS - Pearson Education, 2004.

[25] J. P. Guilford, 'Creativity', *American Psychologist*, vol. 5, no. 9, pp. 444–454, 1950, doi: 10.1037/h0063487.

[26] E. P. Torrance, 'Relationships with creative talent', *Guiding Creative Talent*, Englewood Cliffs, NJ: Prentice-Hall, Inc., 1962, pp. 162–187, doi: 10.1037/13134-009.

[27] A. Osborn, *Applied Imagination: Principles and Procedures of Creative Problem Solving*, New York: Charles Scribner's Sons, 1953.

[28] Paul B. Paulus and Bernard A. Nijstad, *Group Creativity: Innovation through Collaboration*, New York: Oxford University Press, 2003, pp. xiii, 346.

[29] S. Parnes, 'Education and creativity', in *Creativity: Its Educational Implications*, New York: Wiley, 1967.

[30] B. Eberle, *Scamper: Games for Imagination Development*, Waco, TX: Prufrock Press, 1996.

[31] E. De Bono, *Po: Beyond Yes & No.* New York: Penguin Books, 1973.

[32] G. Kalmpourtzis, 'Teaching of spatial thinking in early childhood through game-based learning: The use of the iPad', in *Proceedings of the European Conference on Games-based Learning*, 2014, vol. 1, pp. 231–239 [Online], http://www.scopus.com/inward/record.url?eid=2-s2.0-84923545495&partnerID=40&md5=4981404690aeb1450e06f043ab252200.

[33] G. Kalmpourtzis, 'Connecting game design with problem posing skills in early childhood', *British Journal of Educational Technology*, vol. 50, no. 2, pp. 846–860, 2019, doi: 10.1111/bjet.12607.

[34] G. Kalmpourtzis, 'Developing kindergarten students' game design skills by teaching game design through organized game design interventions', *Multimedia Tools and Applications*, vol. 78, pp. 1–26, 2019.

[35] M. Romero and G. Kalmpourtzis, 'Constructive alignment in game design for learning activities in higher education', *Information*, vol. 11, no. 3, p. 126, Feb. 2020, doi: 10.3390/info11030126.

[36] E. Sanchez, E. Sanchez, G. Kalmpourtzis, J. Cazes, and M. Berthoix, 'Learning with tactileo map : from gamification to ludicization of fieldwork', *GI Forum*, vol. 1, no. 1, pp. 261–271, 2015, doi: 10.1553/giscience2015s261.

[37] G. Kalmpourtzis, L. Vrysis, and A. Veglis, 'Teaching game design to students of the early childhood through Forest Maths', in *2016 11th International Workshop on Semantic and Social Media Adaptation and Personalization (SMAP)*, Thessaloniki, Greece, Oct. 2016, pp. 123–127, doi: 10.1109/SMAP.2016.7753396.

[38] G. Kalmpourtzis, M. Romero, C. D. Smet, and A. Veglis, 'An analysis for the identification of use and development of game design strategies as problem posing activities for early childhood learners', *Interactive Mobile Communication, Technologies and Learning*, pp. 57–68.

[39] G. Kalmpourtzis, G. Ketsiakidis, L. Vrysis, and M. Romero, 'Examining the impact of an interactive storytelling platform on educational contexts through contemporary crowdsourcing methods of audiovisual content publishing', in *2020 15th International Workshop on Semantic and Social Media Adaptation and Personalization (SMA)*, Zakynthos, Greece, Oct. 2020, pp. 1–5, doi: 10.1109/SMAP49528.2020.9248471.

[40] G. Kalmpourtzis, M. Romero, C. De Smet, and A. Veglis, 'An analysis for the identification of use and development of game design strategies as problem posing activities for early childhood learners', in *Internet of Things, Infrastructures and Mobile Applications*, vol. 1192, M. E. Auer and T. Tsiatsos, Eds., Cham: Springer International Publishing, 2021, pp. 57–68. doi: 10.1007/978-3-030-49932-7_6.

[41] G. Kalmpourtzis, L. Vrysis, and G. Ketsiakidis, 'The role of adults in giving and receiving feedback for game design sessions with students of the early childhood', *Interactive Mobile Communication, Technologies and Learning*, vol. 725, pp. 266–275, 2018.

[42] G. Kalmpourtzis and M. Romero, 'Artifactual affordances in playful robotics', in *Games and Learning Alliance*, vol. 12517, I. Marfisi-Schottman, F. Bellotti, L. Hamon, and R. Klemke, Eds., Cham: Springer International Publishing, 2020, pp. 316–325.

Index

abstracting, thinking tool 192
account organizational complexity
    119–121
actors, journey maps 196
adaptability 100–101
Agile software development
    approaches 35
analogizing 192
analytical thinking 81
appropriateness 60–62
assessment 245–246
audience 134–136

Biggest Design Secret 43–44
    Build–Measure–Learn feedback loop
        50–51
    Design sprints 52
    Design Thinking 53–56
    Dewey's model of problem solving 45
    Double Diamond framework 49–50

George Polya's problem-solving
    process 47
Osborn-Parnes creative problem-
    solving model 48
Torrance's process model 47
Wallas' four stages 45
blog article 27
body thinking 192–193
brainstorming 36, 202–206
broader processes 86–87, 167–168
building teams 133
Build–Measure–Learn feedback loop
    50–51
Build phase 51
bus accident paradigm 244–245
business objectives 136–138

capturing questions 189–190
card-sorting activity 36
Carvel, T. 184

collective memory 110–114
comfort zone 170
communication 62–65
continuous design approximations 231
convergent thinking 215–216
    about consensus and voting
        220–221
    assessing ideas 216–220
    co-creation 221–222
    divergent 222–223
creative pauses 208–209
creative stakeholders 14–17, 167,
        168–171, 190
    field experts 134
    individuals 133–134
creativity 16, 45, 149
    Torrance's process model 47

designers 3
design processes
    account organizational complexity
        119–121
    activities 35–38, 84, 85
    activity sets 85–86
    adaptability 100–101
    analytical and synthetical thinking
        80–82
    assessment 245–246
    break silos and encourage
        co-creation 114–116
    broader processes 86–87
    categorize and address problems
        39–42
    collective memory 110–114
    creating 21–23, 78–80
    efficiency improvement 122
    excuses 24–28
    feasibility and innovation 109–110
    five questions 130–132, 144–145
    form of process 34–35
    human-centered processes 106–108
    intrinsically motivating 154–156
    journey maps 195–198
    levels of focus 87–91
    linearity *vs.* nonlinearity 127–128
    mitigation strategies 123–124
    narratives 193
    number and granularity of steps
        94–100
    personas 194–195

phase 102
problem finding and problem solving
        18–21, 82–84
problems 8
representation 124
scalability 100–101
sequences 102–106
setting up 250
short-and long-term outcomes
        117–118
straight lines *vs.* circles and loops
        125–126
team size 91–94
test 230
user research 110–114
Design Process Rectangle 44, 54, 72, 86,
        99, 180
design sprints 52
design team transition 167–168
design thinking 53–56
detaching play from design 149–153
developers 3
Dewey, J. 45
Dewey's Model of problem solving 45
dimensional thinking 193
divergent thinking strategies 200–202
    brainstorming 202–206
    creative pauses 208–209
    mental barriers remove 211–215
    SCAMPER 206–208
    "What Ifs" 209–210
domain context 138–140
Double Diamond framework 49–50

e-commerce website 80
effective design processes 23, 29–30
emergent problems 39
empathizing, Design Thinking 193
encouraging innovation 23
existent problems 39
extrinsic motivation 154, 155

facilitating communication 23
fear of failure 149
feasibility 109–110
flexible design processes 23
forming patterns 192
forming phase 166
Four Fundamental Phases 43,
        55–56, 180

George Polya's problem-solving
    process 47
Global Positioning System (GPS)
    tracking systems 110
good time-keeping 174–175
Google Ventures 52
granularity 95, 97, 98

high-fidelity prototypes 230–231
human-centered process 58
    creative delivery 72
    creativity 59–65
    design processes (*see* design
        processes)
    embrace error 68–70
    encourage personal development
        74–76
    human thought 65–67
    memory 72–74
    team stability 71

ice-breaker game 36
ideation 37, 48, 53
ill-defined problems 40, 41
illumination, creative processes 45
imaging 192
implementation 226–229
incubation, creative processes 45
industry-established processes 250
intrinsically motivating design processes
    23, 154, 155

Jarman, B. 148
journey maps 195–198
"jukebox" 3

Land, G. 148
Lean Startup methodology 50, 55–56
learning 75
Learn phase 56
linearity *vs.* nonlinearity 127–128
linear processes 102–103
long-term goals 186, 187
low-fidelity prototypes 230

McKee, R. 180
meaningful design processes 23
Measure phase 56
memorable moments 12
Minimum Viable Product (MVP) 50

modeling 193
modern product design 15
multinational corporation 3–4
MVP *see* Minimum Viable Product
    (MVP)

nonlinear processes 103–105
norming phase 166–167

observation 192
onsite work configurations 141–143
originality 59
Osborn-Parnes creative problem-solving
    (CPS) model 48

panic zone 171
pauses 175; creative 208–209
performing phase 167
personas 194–195
physical proximity 141
Piaget, J. 156
play 156–160, 193
    autotelic 156
    flow 158–160
    pleasure 158
    stress 160–161
    surprises 158
Polya, G. 47
potential problems 39–40
pragmatic design processes 23
preparation, creative processes 45
problem finding 184–185
    capturing questions 189–190
    clearly communicate process goals
        186–187
    facilitate 185–186
    intrinsically motivating 18–21
    present and capitalize on user
        research 188
    thirteen thinking tools 192–193
problem-solving process 47
    intrinsically motivating 18–21
process breakdown 196
prototyping phase, Design
    Thinking 55

recognizing patterns 192
remote work configurations 141–142
resources 141
Ries, E. 50

Root-Bernstein, M. 192
Root-Bernstein, R. 192

scalability 100–101
SCAMPER 206–208
scenario, journey maps 196
Schell, J. 158
short-term goals 186
solution
    application 226–229
    approximation 231
    assessment 234
    exploring 229–230
    prototypes 230–231
Sparks of Genius (Root-Bernstein and
       Root-Bernstein)
storming phase 166
stretching zone 171
synthesizing, thinking tool 193
synthetical thinking 80–82

team building 23, 165
team dynamics 171–173
    timing 174–175

test, Design Thinking 54, 230
thirteen thinking tools 192–193
Torrance, E.P. 47; process model of
      creativity 47
transforming, thinking tool 193
Tuckman, B. 166

unsuccessful products 11
usability tests 37, 237–242
User Experience (UX) designers 2
User Interface (UI) designers 2
user research
    present and capitalize on 188
    solution assessment 234–235,
      242–243
user researchers 2

verification, creative processes 45

Wallas, G. 45
well-defined problems 40, 41
"What Ifs" 209–210

Yerkes-Dodson law 160